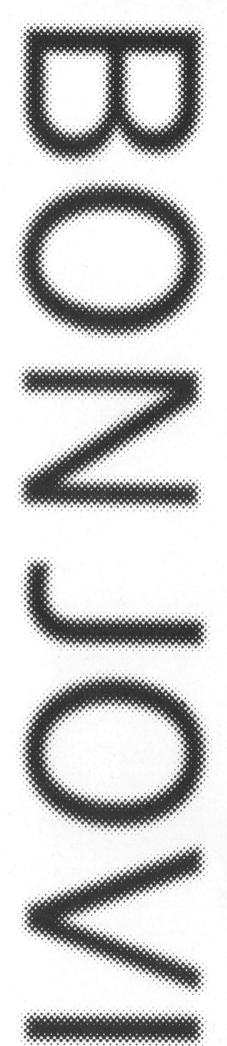

'All Night Long'... The True Story of BON JOVI by Mick Wall

 **OMNIBUS PRESS**

London/New York/Paris/Sydney

Copyright © 1995 Omnibus Press.
(A Division of Book Sales Limited)

Edited by Chris Charlesworth.
Cover & book designed by
Michael Bell Design.
Picture research by Nikki Russell.

ISBN 0.7119.4894.1
Order No.OP47765

Exclusive distributors:
Book Sales Limited
8/9 Frith Street, London W1V 5TZ, UK.

Music Sales Corporation
257 Park Avenue South, New York,
NY 10010, USA.

Music Sales Pty Limited
120 Rothschild Avenue, Rosebery,
NSW 2018, Australia.

To the Music Trade only:
Music Sales Limited
8/9 Frith Street, London W1V 5TZ, UK.

Photo credits: Aki/Retna: 52, 56;
Edie Baskin/Retna: 80b, 84t&b; Garry
Brandon/Redferns: 42; Larry Busacca/
Retna: front cover, 32b, 60b, 70, 75, 76b,
81tl, 82t, 85b, 88b, 88/89, 91t, 92l&r,
93; Mike Cameron/Redferns: 30, 59; EJ
Camp/Retna: 9t, 16, 20; Dominick Conde/
StarFile: 71; Kieran Doherty/Redferns: 83;
Douglas Brothers/Retna: 86; George J.
Gobes/StarFile: 27, 58t, 62b; Steve
Granitz/Retna: 51b; Adrian Green/Retna:
44b; Bob Gruen/StarFile: 40, 47, 54b;
Mark Harlan/StarFile: 7b; Mick Hutson/
Redferns: 40b, 73r, 85t, 89t; JJ/StarFile:
26, 34t, 62t; Michael Johansson/Retna:
17t, 29; Todd Kaplan/StarFile: back cover
inset, 33l&r, 37, 38, 39, 46, 47b, 49l,
51t, 53; Bob King /Redferns: 16b; Bernard
Kuhmstedt/Retna: back cover; Bob Leafe/
StarFile: 7t; London Features International:
9b, 13, 24, 25, 31, 41, 43, 44t, 48b,
49r, 54t, 60t, 64, 65br, 66, 67t, 69, 72b,
73l, 74t&b, 76, 80, 81br, 82b, 88t, 90t,
96; Jeffrey Lowe/Retna: 60/61, 77;
Michael Malfer/Retna: 5tr; Ross Marino/
Retna: 4; Barry Morgenstein/Retna: 45;
Philip Ollerenshaw/StarFile: 67b; Chuck
Pulin/StarFile: 18, 19, 34b, 48, 50, 79;
Rex Features: back cover, 5tl, 12b,57, 86/
87, 90b; Ebet Roberts/Redferns: 5bl, 8,
10t, 14, 17b, 21, 24b, 28, 32, 35, 36,
58b, 64b, 78b; Phyllis Rosney/StarFile:
23; Lisa Seifert/StarFile: 22; StarFile: 13,
14; Luciano Viti/Retna: 6; Timothy White/
Retna: 65t, 68:

Every effort has been made to trace the
copyright holders of the photographs in this
book but one or two were unreachable.
We would be grateful if the photographers
concerned would contact us.

Printed by Scotprint Limited,
Mussleburgh, Edinburgh, Scotland.

A catalogue record for this book is
available from the British Library.

This book is dedicated to Arnie,
Best bud 'til the end - MW

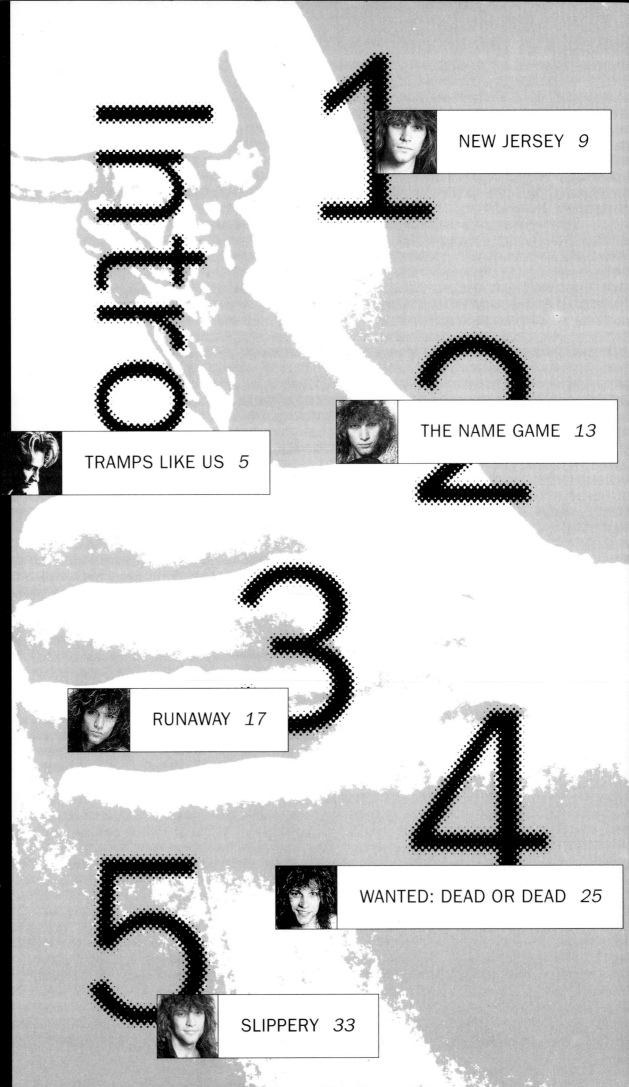

TRAMPS LIKE US

give in. With the seats less than a quarter full when Bon Jovi hit the stage, the singer in the too-tight pants and far too much eye make-up played it like he'd just stepped out on stage to wall-to-wall screaming bodies.

Just 22 years old, he was still giving it loads of that 'I'm just a kid in a candy store' schtick that he thought was cute in those days, but straight away you could tell that there was going on behind those watchful brown eyes than a few hackneyed old rock and roll riffs.

Over the next 10 years, we met and talked on several occasions, recording interviews whose extracts were broadcast or published in a variety of media-guises, from shows I presented on Sky TV, Radio 1 and Capital Radio, to a host of different magazines and newspapers around the world. Along the way, I watched a sharp-eyed youth with a nice line in self-deprecating humour grow into a man of considerable accomplishments; a wiser, more serious-minded musician who makes it a point of principle these days to always look a gift horse in the mouth.

From the word go, it was plain that Jon always believed in his own ability to make it as a rock and roll singer. But the phenomenal level of success that has become the chief characteristic of his ever-deepening fame was beyond even Jon's own wildest hopes. In 1995, there aren't many people under the age of 30 who don't think they know who Bon Jovi is. Over the last eight years, it has become a household name; the true hallmark of fame being when your mum thinks your favourite records are quite good, too. What I like about Jon, though, is that most people with his looks and talent wouldn't try half so hard as he does to make sure things go right when you meet him, wouldn't try even a quarter as hard to be so personable and down-to-earth.

In September 1994, *RAW* magazine estimated that Jon was the wealthiest rock star of his generation in the world. Based on total album sales in the region of 34 million, and taking into consideration his share of the takings from concerts, official merchandise, videos, MTV and radio plays, *RAW* estimated that his personal fortune was in the $80 million range. Mind you, that was before 'Always' made another hole in the ozone layer.

Rockwise, long before tattoo-less, adolescent-minded boys discovered the blue-collar lyrical solecisms and ouch-making lead guitar of his biggest hits, the little girls and the marketing men knew best. With tightbuns, full basket, and a face as cute as a puppy, Bon Jovi went supernova in Japan before anywhere else; and that was with their first single, 'Runaway'. Which says more about Japan's taste in rock bands than it does about Bon Jovi's early records.

Jon's no bimbo, though. You want to talk to the man in charge of all things Bon Jovi, you talk to Jon – there's no other choice. He runs the show, because he's the one, ultimately, who takes the responsibility for its success or failure. Everyone has their part to play, of course, but Jon is the only one who is truly irreplaceable. Fully aware of the fact that the band bears his name, photo sessions are always personally sifted through

The first time I met Jon Bon Jovi was in 1984, when Bon Jovi toured Britain for the first time, supporting Kiss. I saw the show at Wembley Arena in London and it was clear that a young star was in the making. The songs hadn't arrived yet – everything sounded like it was written earlier that day – but the force and confidence of the performance was striking. In those days Kiss was still something of a legend in the UK and very few of the kids there that night gave a shit about the support band. But this kid just didn't

for the shots Jon prefers; recording sessions don't begin or end until Jon says so; every piece of merchandise from Bon Jovi baseball caps and wristbands to the finished albums themselves, anything that bears the official 'Bon Jovi' stamp, has come with Jon's personal seal of approval.

In the early days, despite numerous requests, he would refuse interviews with teeny magazines like *Sassy*, in the US, or *Smash Hits*, in the UK, because he desperately wanted his band to be taken seriously. "I told my record company that if they tried to do that I'd go crazy," he told me in 1985. With the first 'Bon Jovi' album, he deliberately "played down the looks of this band to death. I have to live with myself as a performer first. I have to know when I wake up in the morning if the people bought the record because it was a great song or if it was because I'm a pin-up. That whole scene would kill me, it really would..."

In time, of course, he realised that such crucial matters as his favourite colour or what kind of girls he likes to date are an important part of his job, as is explaining to some weird-haired scribe from the rock press the 'true meaning' behind a song like 'Keep The Faith'. After you've sold your first 10 million records there isn't anything left to be asked that doesn't begin to sound strange.

Always in demand, always on the go, the shocking truth about Jon Bon Jovi is that what you see is usually what you get. Or as close to it as you're ever likely to find yourself in this new age of pop stars with symbols instead of names and video bands with dance routines instead of songs.

At ease in the company of other celebrities, Jon is on first name terms with Elton, with Emilio, even with Big Frank (Bruno). Nothing unusual about that, of course. Fame likes fame and, in public, celebrities are usually drawn together. There's safety in the light. What is unusual about a star of the magnitude of Jon Bon Jovi is that he still knows all the names of the faces that will never be famous. He still has time to stop and say hello to people less successful artists don't even bother saying good-bye to: the behind-the-sceners, the fans who arrive early and leave late on the off chance Jon might suddenly materialise before them for a few seconds, the bloke who's been driving him around for the last three days.

Yes, I'm afraid it's true, Jon Bon Jovi is a genuinely nice guy. But that doesn't mean he's a saint. Far from it. He doesn't suffer fools gladly and he has his bad hair days just like the rest of us, sometimes worse than the rest of us, maybe, after 36 straight hours in the studio, or maybe 36 non-stop weeks on the road. And of course, just like the rest of us, sometimes for no apparent reason. Which, after all, is only proof that, whatever else he has become, Jon Bon Jovi remains thankfully human.

Until he decides to tell it the way he remembers it himself – and I wouldn't advise you hold your breath waiting – if you want to know the truth about Jon Bon Jovi, this is it...

Mick Wall, February 1995.

*Top: Jon with The Rest:
never truly credible.*

" I'd have played a pay toilet and used my own change! "

NEW JERSEY

" You have to cite Bruce and the whole Jersey scene I grew up in as all being a heavy influence on my career, it was because of those guys I played the guitar. "

" Ultimately, I don't really want to be anybody other than who I already am. "

*Below: Jon in his
High School days.*

John Bongiovi Junior was born on March 2, 1962, in Perth Amboy, New Jersey, about 25 miles north of Asbury Park, neo-mythical home of New Jersey's most famous rock son, Bruce Springsteen. The eldest, eventually, of three sons (Anthony and Matt soon followed), born to Carol and John Bongiovi Snr, John's main characteristic as a child, according to his mother, was that "he liked to show off". Of course, Carol would always jokingly add that the extrovert side of her son's personality came from her side of the family. In her own youth, she had always been regarded as a good-looking, talented girl; once she was crowned Miss Erie, Pennsylvania, and had worked briefly after that as a Playboy Bunny.

When John Jnr. revealed to her his own dreams of becoming a full-time entertainer, it was Carol, in particular, who went out of her way to encourage him. Carol understood that sort of dream; she has lived with an unfulfilled version of it all her life. It wasn't a case

of pushing her son unduly, she always maintained, but once he'd made up his mind, her support was crucial.

As for John Snr., he had harboured singing ambitions of his own in his early years, though he never mentioned it now, and he was prepared to sit back and see just how far his boy's dreams took him before he decided it was time to maybe talk some goddamn sense into him. These days Carol helps run the Bon Jovi fan club and is clearly immensely proud of her son's achievements, while John Snr. is liable to pop up in the backstage area, where his talents as a host are matched only by the huge smile with which he greets his son's guests. He's no longer waiting to have that talk, though.

When John was four, the family moved to a house in Sayreville, New Jersey. Little John got his first guitar when he was seven, bought for him by his mother. But in typical infant style, the future rock star showed more interest in playing with the case the guitar came in than the instrument itself. It was another three years, in fact, before John got round to picking it up and strumming it. Suddenly, curious about pop music and its dramatic effect on teenage girls, John began to take occasional lessons from a local music teacher, Al Parinello.

"You have to cite Bruce and the whole Jersey scene I grew up in as all being a heavy influence on my career," he says. "It was because of those guys I played guitar. It wasn't because of The Beatles. I was only three years of age when they came to America. My mother listened to The Beatles...

"You've got to figure, in '75 when 'Born To Run' hit, I was 13! That's when I first got into rock'n'roll. That was one of the first albums I ever bought... that and 'Caribou' by Elton John and all the Thin Lizzy albums, all that kind of stuff. I thought I was cool because I dug The Animals in 1975 when nobody in Jersey my age had ever heard of them...

"So, all those guys, particularly the New Jersey bands, were a big, big influence on where I come from, musically. When I might get hit on for it by critics, I have to own up and say, yeah, I'm guilty of being influenced by some of these people like Southside Johnny or Little Steven – both of whom were as important to me as Bruce. But, really, so what?

"They never bother to also point out that Bruce copped a lot of his early inspiration from listening to Bob Dylan records. Or that Dylan lifted one or two of his big ideas from Woody Guthrie... I mean, where do you draw the line? The fact of the matter is everybody grows up wanting to be someone else, one of their heroes. Keith Richards grew up wanting to be Chuck Berry, and look what happened to him. All Little Steven wants to be when he grows up is Keith Richards! And Bruce wants to be Dylan and we want to be Bruce...

"It's all so ridiculous. Ultimately, I don't really want to be anybody other than who I already am. But those influences remain constant. I prefer to look on it as added spice in the pot. No more, no less..."

His first proper get-up-and-show-everybody band was called Starz, formed with friends from high-school, but they never got past their first gig after somebody

NEW JERSEY

told them there was already a more established American band called Starz. Going with the flow, John changed the name to Raze. Raze played their first ever gig at a talent contest at Sayreville High, where most of the band were still pupils. They performed their songs: 'Strutter' by Kiss, Chuck Berry's 'Johnny B. Goode' and 'Taking Care Of Business' by Bachman-Turner Overdrive. It was not a life-changing experience. Raze came last. "Start at the bottom, they say, don't they?" he once laughingly recalled. "Well, I sure did that..."

It was while he was at Sayreville High that John toyed with an acting career, appearing in a provincial theatre version of the hit stage musical *Mame*. John played Junior Babcock, a small role but a significant step that stood him in good stead when, years later, he was offered another small part, albeit somewhat more prestigious, in the film *Young Guns II*, for which he also wrote the title song. As Jon Bon Jovi, rock star, he has always denied having any serious interest in becoming a movie star, but at the end of 1995 he will be seen making his silver screen début in a major role, that of painter Valentino in the romantic comedy *Moonlight & Valentino*, alongside Elizabeth Perkins and Whoopi Goldberg.

Jon would also audition for the lead role in the musical *Footloose*. "Paramount Pictures took me out to see if I wanted to play the lead (in *Footloose*)," Jon told me when we first met. "They couldn't find a kid who could dance well enough, so they were gonna change the story to a kid who was struggling to be a rock star instead of wanting to be a dancer. It was about three or four months before our first album came out and they asked me if I would be interested. But I turned down the chance because what I really wanted to be known for was making records, and if I made it in a movie first then forever more I would be labelled as an actor that wanted to be a rock star, and I said no, this is wrong." Based on the history of chronic incompatibility between rock stars and the silver screen, this was a shrewd judgement.

Back in the late Seventies, John Jnr. was still busy plotting a more serious successor to Raze. With classmate Willy Hercek, he put together a band called The Atlantic City Expressway (known around town simply as ACE), an ambitious R&B ten-piece which began life playing at local parties. It provided John with his first taste of the real thing, gigging for nickels and dimes in smoky bars and late-night one-stops dotted along the Jersey coastline.

Among the musicians in ACE was David Rashbaum, a young classically-trained keyboard player looking for something "a little more kick ass than Schubert" to see out his teens. Soon to change his name to David Bryan, he was born on February 7, 1962, in Edison, New Jersey, and trained as a classical pianist since he was seven years old. He had played in a fairly well-known local covers band called Transition before signing on with John in ACE. "There wasn't anything difficult about what he was doing, but it was

just exciting watching him do it," David once told me. "If there is such a thing as 'star quality', then this guy has it all."

ACE built up a fair-sized local following, playing anywhere and anytime anybody asked them. Their attitude was simple but effective. "I'd have played a pay toilet and used my own change!" Jon would joke years later. But the intention was serious: to get the ball rolling, not wait for someone to tell you it was all right, just do it.

Around this time John began to feel confident about the material he was writing himself and to start including one or two of the more obvious crowd pleasers in the set, casually augmenting the usual staple of 'Born To Run' and 'Brown Sugar' with some of his own tunes. Slowly, ACE were getting noticed. Local celebrities like Southside Johnny (of Asbury Jukes fame and a major inspiration for John), began to show up at the tiny dates they were playing. Even Springsteen himself began turning up and, on more than one breathless occasion, actually got up on stage and jammed with them! Things, surely, did not get any better than this...

In fact, as far as ACE was concerned, they really didn't. World-beating as those nights when Bruce joined in might have seemed, the end for ACE came swiftly when David Rashbaum left to enrol in the renowned Juilliard School Of Music in New York City (the original funky-playground on which the film and TV show *Fame* was based), and John quickly followed suit. A keyboard player they could replace, but without their figurehead and main source of frantic energy, ACE disintegrated on the spot.

Now in his late teens and desperate to get a new handle on things, John teamed up for a while with The Rest, a local punk band. Something of a departure for him, The Rest was built around the not inconsiderable talents of guitarist/songwriter Jack Ponti, who in later years would make a name for himself writing and producing for chart-hoppers like Michael Bolton and Nelson. The Rest didn't really have what it took to make it as a credible punk outfit but Ponti, to his credit, recognised that he did not have John's unusual charisma, and recruiting to the band soon had the desired effect on the The Rest's immediate prospects. Both Billy Squier (a huge star in the US in those days) and Southside Johnny produced demos for the band. They even attracted interest from Capitol and Columbia Records, but neither shark eventually bit.

The gigs did keep coming, though, the most memorable being the afternoon The Rest played at The Freehold Raceway in New Jersey, opening up on a bill that also included Hall & Oates and Southside Johnny & The Asbury Jukes. Over 20,000 fans turned up – young John's first experience of a stadium-sized crowd! Nevertheless, with no sign of a record deal on the horizon, John began to get itchy feet. The end came when he was fired by Ponti, but the moment John was out of the picture the band simply fell apart. "I was young and if any of those early bands I sang in had made it, I'd probably still be there," he later recalled.

History, though, had other plans.

Tico (top), Alec (centre) and Richie (bottom).

THE NAME GAME

❝ I was just some shithead gofer with a tape. ❞

❝ For two years I slept on the floor at the studio and just tried my best to learn as much as I could about the music business. ❞

John's second cousin, Tony Bongiovi, owned The Power Station studios in New York, where many top artists had recorded important albums over the years. Regarded throughout the music industry as a first-rate record producer, Tony Bongiovi had seen The Rest in action during 1980 and liked what he saw.

Ask Jon today and he'll tell you that Tony hated The Rest, but in September 1980 he accepted an offer of a small retainer to work at The Power Station as an 'artist in development'. Whether Tony was genuinely trying to help out a promising young talent, or merely giving a job to a member of the family who needed a break, is anybody's guess, but there's no doubt that John Snr. had a few words in Tony's receptive ear. Being an 'artist in development', however, meant that John had to undertake any number of menial tasks. "Make the coffee, go to the liquor store, sweep the floors, I just did whatever I was told," he says now.

"For two years I slept on the floor at the studio and just tried my best to learn as much as I could about the music business. I mean, OK, I got all the shitty jobs, but how many young guys get to sweep the floors and take out the trash for The Rolling Stones, you know what I mean?"

In his new role as Johnny Gofer, John met many of the stars who checked in at The Power Station. He was paid $52.50 per week for his efforts, although this rose to $125 by the time of his departure. More importantly, the fledgling recording star saw at first hand how records were made. He also received encouragement from some very surprising quarters...

"When I was a gofer there, Mick Jagger was very nice to me. The second time he came in he remembered me enough to say, 'You keeping up those demos? You keep on it'. I never forgot that. Maybe that's a part of the reason I'm here today.

"That was a buzz 'cos I was just a shithead little gofer with a tape. It was very nice of him, you know, you don't forget. To have that kind of attention, even when you knew he was just being nice to some kid in the studio, it really made you want to make the best demo ever!"

As an 'artist in development' John could record his own songs during 'down time', the quiet hours before dawn when none of the regular paying customers were using the studios. Working in this way, he cut hour-after-hour of tape. With no permanent band to back him, he either grabbed hold of whoever was around to help out, or else played on his own in the half-light of studio quietude. Eventually, though, a semi-permanent line-up gradually assembled round the young singer. John even gave them a name: The Lechers. Playing live only occasionally, their chief focus was on breaking in John's original material. But with constant line-up changes, The Lechers was never likely to last long.

The next band he put together, however, was almost the real thing. Bursting with brash, bold youth made palatable by clean melodic edges, The Wild Ones could be described, in fact, as the earliest incarnation of Bon Jovi. David Rashbaum returned to the fold, and an old school chum of John's, Dave 'Snake' Sabo, played guitar. The rhythm section was unstable, but the basis had now been laid.

The first song John wrote with this band was called 'Runaway'. It was 1982 and the prevailing trend in American rock was the keyboard-heavy adult-oriented million-sellers like Journey, Styx and REO Speedwagon, all of whom topped the charts in the US that year. Built around a repetitive keyboard riff topped off with lung-bursting choruses and a straight-off-the-peg guitar break, 'Runaway' fitted easily into the mould.

"The first time you heard 'Runaway' it had 'hit' written all over it," recalled future BJ guitarist Richie Sambora, who didn't play on any of the original versions. "I, personally, found it a little lightweight, but then the stuff I like to listen to, you don't hear on the radio so often. Especially not back then. And that was the thing about 'Runaway'... it was instantly one of those songs you knew would sound good on the radio. If it hadn't been released by an unknown band, if Journey or one of those bands had released it, it would have been number one, no problem."

Richie wasn't the only one who felt like that. Tony Bongiovi, sensing perhaps that his investment was about to start paying off, used his own contacts to hurriedly assemble a professional line-up to record the song at The Power Station. Soon, every major record company on the east coast of America received a copy of the tape, credited to 'Johnny B', with three other original tracks. Years later, Jon cannot remember what else was on that demo... or maybe he just doesn't want to recall? Whatever, the only other track that would be known to today's Bon Jovi fan would be 'She Don't Know Me' which, like 'Runaway', ended up on the first Bon Jovi album.

The labels liked what they heard and wanted to see Johnny B perform live. A showcase was set up at The Ritz in New York and yet another new line-up of The Wild Ones was thrown together. David Rashbaum was back in the band and 'Snake' Sabo played lead guitar, but John was forced into using a stand-in rhythm section that had neither the style nor the experience to give him the punch he needed to get his music across. The showcase proved disastrous. Opening for Southside Johnny, it was, John would later confess, "One of the all-time worst shows I've ever done. Everything went wrong. Not one thing. Everything..."

The labels agreed and over Christmas 1982 John Jnr had the queasy feeling his world had gone all the way back to square one.

Tony Bongiovi had been hired to produce a Woolworth's-style festive-season quickie album called 'Star Wars Christmas Album', and John was inveigled into supplying the lead vocal to a track called 'R2D2 – I Wish You A Merry Christmas'. It brought in a little cash, which John used to fund a trip out to California. Accompanied by David Rashbaum, John set his sights on landing a record deal in Los Angeles, home of the industry Big Wheels, and the pair audaciously set up shop in a room at the A-1 Motel in Hollywood.

Their plan was to hit every record label in town with the same tape that had aroused such interest back East. By now, he'd gone back to calling 'the band' The Wild Ones again, having abandoned the idea of Johnny B, which made him sound like a second-rate lounge lizard Lothario. Trouble was, the minute somebody actually stopped what they were doing long enough to admit 'Runaway' sounded like it was born on the radio, they wanted to see The Wild Ones playing live. At that point the conversation tended to tail off.

John needed a stroke of good luck, and he found it back in New York. Unknown to him, an assistant engineer (and aspiring manager) at The Power Station, Ray Willhard, had entered a tape of 'Runaway' in a local radio station talent contest which went under the name of Rock To Riches. Organised by a recently launched (but now defunct) classic-rock station WAPP out on Long Island, the quality of the tape ensured that 'Runaway' walked away with the regional heat of the contest, and John et al were offered the chance to have the track put on a one-off WAPP compilation album, comprised of similar WAPP-sponsored unsigned acts. It was the only offer on the table and John didn't need to be asked twice.

Appearing in early 1983 but commercially available only in the New York State area, the album offered stations owned by WAPP's parent company, Doubleday, gratis tracks for air-play, and 'Runaway' became a regular feature on local radio in the New York tri-state area for almost a month. Also featured on the WAPP compilation were early tracks by Twisted Sister

and Zebra, both of whom would also eventually obtain major record deals. Anybody with a copy of the WAPP album in their closet could probably flog it for a small fortune now.

With 'Runaway' now actually played on the radio, a genuine buzz began to build. Suddenly, after knocking himself out for five years, almost by accident John's music was starting to take on a life of its own. And, as is the norm with the deeply conformist nature of the music industry's talent scouts, the very same record company A&R chiefs – who had only just turned their backs on him after the Ritz fiasco – began now to court John in earnest.

It was around this time that he made the decision to drop the 'Wild Ones' monicker and present himself simply as a solo artist. With the exception of Dave Rashbaum, he had no real band members to flesh-out any potential line-up, and he was firmly against risking everything again by putting on another farcical 'showcase' gig with a bunch of session men. Instead, John came up with the idea of turning his own name into a band name, cleverly electing to trim it down, to "Americanise" it, from Bongiovi to Bon Jovi. By dropping the 'h' from his Christian name – something he had done periodically at school since he was an adolescent – he had Jon Bon Jovi. It rolled off the tongue and it looked right on paper.

A red hot item on the agenda at almost every A&R meeting in New York, two labels quickly emerged as the front runners to sign Jon Bon Jovi, Atlantic and PolyGram. Both were able to offer enormous financial clout, and both already had an impressive roster of artists. An increasingly experienced hand at dealing with the corporate machine, Jon decided to play it cool and try to get the labels bidding against each other. He already had a shrewd idea which one he felt would offer him his best opportunity; now it was merely a question of not hurrying things along too quickly, as he had tried to do in the past, but to wait and see how far up the labels would raise their offers before he made his move.

In the end, PolyGram won because Jon trusted the musicianly background of the man who signed him, an Englishman named Derek Shulman. A former pro-musician in his own right, Shulman had played with early Seventies prog-rockers Gentle Giant, before moving into artist management and eventually his own office at PolyGram in New York. Recognising a like-mind, perhaps, Shulman had every confidence that Jon Bon Jovi was going to be a big star one day. His songs – so far – were catchy enough, if still fairly pedestrian, but he had the looks, the charisma and, even more important, the determination. The two liked each other and got on immediately.

Shulman landed his fish on July 1, 1983, the day Jon inked his solo deal with PolyGram... and celebrated by buying himself a brand new sports car, as well as treating his mom and dad to a holiday. Electing to withdraw from the 'Rock To Riches' final just prior to signing his recording deal, it seemed like Jon had finally got things the way he wanted. It was to be a feeling he would become increasingly used to as

66 My dream was never about
being this big solo star, it was always more
about being in this kind of
band-gang thing, you know **99**

RUNAWAY

Richie:
66 He was charismatic,
he was already a great
frontman. The band was
kicking... **99**

66 Oh, man my main memory is
of people throwing shit at us. **99**

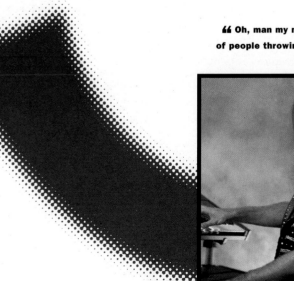

The next step was to put together a new working line-up. Now he could afford to pay wages, Jon was especially keen to surround himself with musicians he could get on with personally. "My dream was never about being this big solo star," he said. "It was always more about being in this kind of band-gang thing, you know?" David Rashbaum was already on board. Next came bass player Alec John Such.

Although he would shed several years in the 'official' Bon Jovi biography first put together by PolyGram, Alec was born on November 14, 1952. Previously he'd made a living by combining studio session work with playing in any number of faceless New Jersey cover bands. Alec lost no time in suggesting bringing in his pal, drummer Hector 'Tico' Torres. Born on October 7, 1953, Tico was a road-hardened studio veteran who had performed on numerous albums throughout the years, often uncredited. At the time, he was earning his keep in a band called Frankie And The Knockouts, then signed to RCA.

They had released several albums which caused minor ripples in train-spotterish AOR circles, but perhaps the most interesting thing about Frankie And The Knockouts was the fact that they were managed by Burt Ward, better known for his green tights and yellow cape while playing Robin The Boy Wonder in the camp cult Sixties TV series *Batman*. 'Frankie' was Frankie Previtt, who was to later win an Oscar for the original music in the quintessential Eighties movie, *Dirty Dancing*.

Dave 'Snake' Sabo was still on lead guitar, but deep inside Jon knew this arrangement wouldn't work in the long term. The ideal guitarist, who would eventually become Jon's second-lieutenant in the band, turned up on the invitation of Alec and Tico at a New Jersey club gig.

Richard Stephen Sambora was born in Woodbridge, New Jersey on July 11, 1959. Like Jon, he came from an entertainment background; both his parents were prize-winning ballroom dancers. Teaching himself to play guitar from an early age, he was also encouraged to take regular piano lessons. By the age of 11, Richie was an accomplished multi-instrumentalist. He could play guitar, piano, accordion and trumpet; and he could sing. It was no surprise in the Sambora household when his first semi-pro band, Mercy, which he formed as a teenager, were signed to Led Zeppelin's then newly-formed Swan Song label. "Apart from Zeppelin themselves, the only other band on the label with Mercy was Bad Company, and their album had just gone to No. 1," he told me.

Mercy was a heavily stylised progressive-rock band, rather too heavily influenced by the theatrical mysticism of Yes and Pink floyd, but laced with the more earthy blues-dominated swagger of Led Zeppelin. Richie was a big fan of Zep guitarist Jimmy Page. "Of course, I've met him many times now and I know what a nice, normal guy he is away from the stage," says Richie. "But, man, the minute he straps on his guitar, I'm transformed into a huge fan again! I'm still in awe of him."

Swan Song lost interest in Mercy before they got around to releasing anything, and the label petered out when a series of tragedies, culminating in John Bonham's death, hit Led Zeppelin in the late Seventies. Next, Richie joined a funk band called Duke Williams And The Extremes, signed to Macon based Capricorn Records. But their style – 'fusion' funk-metal – was about as fashionable as flares in the early Eighties. After being offered a small role (playing the part of a musician) in the film *Staying Alive*, Richie flirted with becoming a jobbing actor but abandoned the idea the first time somebody offered him a job playing guitar somewhere.

In 1983, when Alec and Tico, whom Richie knew through the session-circuit, persuaded Richie to come down and check out their new band, the guitarist had just finished a stint on the road supporting Joe Cocker in a band called The Message. "That was when I decided I couldn't do it alone, I needed another smart person to help me get where I wanted to be, which wasn't doing sessions, but writing and playing in my own band," Richie told the author.

The first time Richie saw Jon on stage, he was so impressed he went straight backstage afterwards and told him there and then that he was the guitarist Jon was looking for. "I went to see them play in a club in Jersey, and I walked in and I knew straight away," Richie recalled. "Actually, Kiss had called me up to do an audition with them in Los Angeles (Richie was on the short list to replace Vinnie Vincent). But with Jon... after the show, I walked right up and introduced myself, I gave him a verbal resumé, and said I had a lot of songs and I had knowledge of making records, and that the guitar player was very good but he was very young."

As luck would have it, Jon had more or less already decided that it wasn't going to work with his childhood friend Dave Sabo, who would later find recognition with Skid Row. "Jon was ready to make his run, he had it together already," says Richie. "He was charismatic, he was already a great frontman. The band was kicking – and I was the missing piece. I really somehow saw it, and I never did anything like that before in my life. I really walked straight up to Jon and went, 'Hi, I'm Richie Sambora, here I am, blah blah blah'.

"He was a bit funny at first, you know, he kinda shrugged me off a little bit. But then a week later I got a call and I went into rehearsal with them. It's funny, it's almost like fate. I look at it that way. Jon was late and by the time he got there, I had the band like this," snaps fingers. "I mean, whipped up and grooving. Jon walked in, listened for about 30 seconds and went 'Hired!'."

With a completed line-up now in place, the only detail that remained was whether to present the package as solo artist-with-backing-band, or push it as a full-blooded band with its own name and shared identity. There were pros and cons either way. Jon was keen on the band idea; his record company didn't care. Jon was the only one actually signed to the label; as long as they were free to promote Jon as a star in his own right, he could call his band whatever he wanted within reason.

In the end, they came up with a solution that satisfied both camps. Victory was a name considered, then thankfully dropped. Johnny Lightning was another awful possibility for a few days. Nothing felt right. In the end, PolyGram's then head of A&R, Jerry Jaffe, came up with the idea of simply using the name Bon Jovi.

The band warmed up by going out on tour to build a momentum. Dubbed 'The Stationwagon Tour', it saw them play, in typical style, everywhere and anywhere that would have them. Nowhere was too small and, for the first time, nowhere was too big either. They even got to play Madison Square Garden, opening up for ZZ Top. Recalling those long gone days, Jon has little sentiment. "When I look back there's nothing I miss from those early days apart from the innocence and fun. It was really hard work."

If things were to work on a business level, then the young band needed proper management to guide them through the minefield of dealing with the record industry and keeping hold of their money. Many a talented band has been blown apart financially and personally because they lacked an experienced manager. Jon wasn't about to make the same mistake.

As it happened several top managers already had their eye on him, and it wasn't long before he signed a management deal with McGhee Entertainment in New York, who also looked after then US mega-stars Mötley Crüe. It was still a new and hungry organisation, but between them, Doc McGhee and his partner, Doug Thaler, had vast experience in the music industry.

On another level Tony Bongiovi, in somewhat cavalier fashion, decided that he would personally oversee production of the first Bon Jovi album proper. Veteran producer Lance Quinn (who also happened to be Tony's partner) was hired to 'help out' in the studio, inevitably The Power Station. The result was a decidedly patchy eponymous début album.

Originally to be released under the huff an' puff title of 'Tough Talk', the album's cover featured a shot of Jon crossing a lamp-lit New York street, staring enigmatically into camera and looking about as threatening as a kitten. In the middle of the road stands a sultry female (or rather, a 1983 American record-sleeve version of sultry; big hair, slit skirt, curvy bum...). The decision to keep things simple and call both band and album 'Bon Jovi' was made by the suits at PolyGram, reflecting where the record company money-men felt the band's best chances of success lay – in Jon himself.

Raved about in melodic hard rock circles on its US release in January 1984 (a European release followed three months later, the only time that a Bon Jovi album wasn't granted simultaneous world-wide release), the music sounded rather stilted and slightly dated. There was a guest performance from Canadian star Aldo Nova, the Montreal-based singer-guitarist who'd briefly broken into the big time with his own début album a couple of years previously and who was brought in to add 'commerciality' to the project. Years later, Jon was to repay Aldo for his help by signing him to his own label when Nova couldn't get arrested elsewhere.

The revamped 'Runaway' (which was to provide the band with their first US Top 40 single, peaking at No. 39, in February 1984) was passable, while 'Breakout' fulfilled all the requirements of a 1984-style 'power ballad'. And both the self-consciously anthemic 'Get Ready', and the straightforward head-snapping 'Shot Through The Heart' are big singalongs.

Whatever its drawbacks, though, the album garnered positive reviews in such bastions of underprivileged rock as *Kerrang!* magazine, in Britain, where their then resident pomp-rock-fixated critic, Paul Suter, claimed somewhat breathlessly that "Jon Bon Jovi has assembled a band of classic finesse and brutal strength... The material is dramatic and energetic, and blessed with a commerciality that should ensure plentiful sales." But, in truth, the début Bon Jovi album was a dull, mediocre affair.

Relentlessly hyped in the consumer rock press, its creator coyly thrust onto the pin-up pages of the teenies and worked to death on the road, the 'Bon Jovi' album eventually reached No. 43 in the US. It only made it as far as No. 71 in the UK charts, chicken feed compared to what would become the norm just two years later, but, hell, it was a beginning, dude. And it sure beat pushing a broom around a room full of people making someone else's music.

Bon Jovi were also swept into the burgeoning video arena with an experimental promotional vid for 'Runaway'. Shot over a period of three days in a disused Jersey warehouse, the result remains an embarrassment to Jon and the band to this day. "Oh, man... that video!" Jon shakes his head whenever reminded of it. "The video for 'Runaway' was just the biggest piece of shit." Jon claimed the producer flat-out refused to even attempt to follow the song's storyline. "He wanted his niece in it in some sort of concept thing that had nothing whatsoever to do with the song. It was awful.

Bon Jovi on the video set for 'Runaway'.

It made us look like assholes, frankly. I was very unhappy about it, but what could I do? It was my first video you know, I was still following instructions, at this point."

The video for 'Runaway' cost Bon Jovi $60,000. The first time this was brought to his attention, he just shrugged. He hadn't discovered yet that the budgets set aside for video and album recordings by record companies, however large, are no more than loans to the artist, against which their share of royalties from record sales are to be eventually paid back. As Jon later confessed to *RAW* magazine: "I learnt a new word that day. The record company lawyer walked right in after we'd watched the video and said, 'Isn't it sooo wonderful?' And we went, 'Yeah!' And he said, 'Yeah, and it's recoupable too!' And I said, 'Great! It's recoupable.' I went outside and said, 'What the fuck does that mean?!' We learnt from our mistakes."

The let-down over the 'Runaway' video notwithstanding, Bon Jovi made rapid progress in establishing themselves as a premier rock outfit of the Eighties. In America, they jumped on tour with various acts, including The Scorpions, during the latter's massive 'Love At first Sting' jaunt. But opening for such a major band wasn't all roses and chocolates. They might have been performing before tens of thousands of fans every night, but few took notice of the raw, young support band. Everyone was there to be rocked by the proverbial Teutonic hurricane and this young, unknown band merely filled in time before the main event. Even worse, in every city they played Bon Jovi found massive displays of Scorpions records in the local stores. The local reps were pushing the easy option of the bill toppers, and the support band were suffering as a result. This wasn't amusing to Jon or Doc McGhee, but they had to bite their tongues and bide their time.

"Oh, man, my main memory is of people throwing shit at us," Richie smiled when I asked him to recall those days. "But that's really the kind of thing that made us a strong band. What we basically learned was that if you stuck together you could be anything."Stuck together? The evidence suggests something other than an all-for-one one-for-all ideology. Richie still had his own personal manager, who was telling all and sundry that he was only leasing out his services to Bon Jovi on a purely temporary basis, and that he had plans for a solo album.

Talking just prior to the band supporting Kiss on their first European tour, Jon nevertheless emphasised just how much he thought they'd improved as a unit. "With The Scorpions we got no soundchecks, minimal stage room and use of the PA rig and the lighting. There were a lot of things working against us. I personally tried to do the best that I could."

Now for their first visit to Britain, they were to tour supporting another rock legend – Kiss, also signed to the PolyGram stable – who are notorious for treating their opening acts with patronising disdain. The shows kicked off on September 30 in Brighton, traversing the country throughout the next two weeks, taking in dates at Southampton, Cornwall, Manchester, Glasgow, Edinburgh, Newcastle, Leicester, Ipswich, Stafford, Leeds and London. The climax of the tour occurred at the Wembley Arena over two nights during mid October – a momentous occasion for the still-inexperienced Bon Jovi boys. And there was little doubt that by the time the band hit the UK, they were considerably improved. Bon Jovi had not only survived this testing trek, but actually grown through the experience. And the fans had warmed to them too.

"The Scorpions were very good to us on our first tour," said Jon later. ".38 Special were real good to us on the 'Slippery...' tour. They were legitimately niceguys, Southside Johnny has always been a great guy. Ten years ago Johnny let me open for him and he's still a great guy."

Wait a minute, though, in 1984, Jon had bemoaned his treatment at the hands of The Scorpions. And Billy Squier also came in for some barbed comments from JBJ because of the manner in which

Jon in his backyard.

he'd treated Bon Jovi when 'Slippery...' was selling faster than any other album in the US; Squier didn't take kindly to being eclipsed by his opening band!

But back in 1984, Bon Jovi were learning lessons fast, certainly in the way you had to win over another band's audience. In the UK, they worked hard to win the curious Kiss crowd over, Jon reaching for every let-me-see-your-hands-I-love-London trick in the book to tease a response out of the Kissheads. They chose their material carefully from their début album, and built a sensible, hard-hitting set. With the news of their success in Britain having spread back to America, it reaffirmed their growing reputation.

It also brought immediate pressure on Bon Jovi to return to the studio to record a second album for which they chose to part company with Tony Bongiovi in circumstances that are still shrouded in mystery. Jon and Tony haven't spoken since. The latter felt that all the hard work and effort he had put into developing Jon's latent talents (not to mention the money that had been spent) deserved a slice of the pie, specifically the publishing. Jon signed a publishing deal with him at the time 'Runaway' was first written, whereby Tony would earn publishing royalties on any songs Jon subsequently wrote. Jon, only 20 at the time, quickly regretted it, and chose now to sever any connections with Tony Bongiovi and The Power Station, with the full backing of his family. He was going to stand on his own two feet and wasn't to be intimidated by previous, ill-conceived agreements.

With Tony Bongiovi out of the picture, Jon turned to Lance Quinn (who had dissolved his partnership with Bongiovi in 1984) to produce the new album. Operations were moved from New York to The Warehouse Studios in Philadelphia, where the band shacked up in a small apartment. However, there were distractions. Both Tico and Alec were going through divorces at the time, and the whole atmosphere was thoroughly miserable.

"In the early days we were still trying to find ourselves," Jon told the author in Dublin in 1988. "We were from New Jersey, all we ever had was a pair of jeans and a leather jacket. If you look at the picture of us on our first album that's what we're wearing – a leather jacket and a pair of jeans. Then all those bands came out, you know, that whole LA thing. And looking back – and I can now – I remember seeing Mötley Crüe and Ratt and whoever, in all these magazines, and they were all doing such huge business while we couldn't get arrested. And I remember thinking you know, we gotta go out and rip up our clothes, we gotta go out and wear make–up, and we gotta go out and get the fake jewellery. This'll make us big.

"It took a while to find ourselves, that's all. I mean, you walk down the street in Jersey wearing make–up, man, you're gonna get your ass kicked! So none of that stuff was really us.

"We toured with Ratt in '85 and they really do live that whole LA kind of thing. And they were doing such big business with their second album and we're still nowhere. And we're saying to ourselves – we're better than this, we're a better band, you know. What the fuck's going on? Maybe we need mascara, you know... And this is not to put those guys down, because we're really good friends now with all those guys from Ratt. But it was an experience it took us time to get over.

"I mean, back in '84, '85 I wouldn't even tell people where I was from, because I was afraid of the Bruce Springsteen comparisons. I'd say we're from America, end of story, you know. We spent those first couple of years running around America trying to find ourselves, but still being afraid to show our real roots.

"In a strange way, though, all the problems that we were encountering at the time, in the end just seemed to make us stronger... we were becoming a real band, in the sense that we were becoming friends, sharing things that we had never shared with anyone else. Tico and Alec were having their domestic difficulties, and I had just broken up with my girlfriend, which meant that I felt like shit a lot of the time. So, some of the songs on the album are pretty sad and miserable."

Yet, there was real emotion and maturity in the songs on '7800 Degrees Fahrenheit'. While there was a happy-go-lucky one-dimensional quality to 'Bon Jovi', this time all those learning and maturing experiences drew out a darker, more articulate side as evinced on 'The Hardest Part Is The Night' (Jon's first credible stab at meaningful lovelorn lyrics), 'Price Of Love' ß∑and 'Only Lonely'.

There is certainly a darkness on '7800...', which took its title from the temperature inside a volcano at the time of eruption. For the first time, here was proof that Bon Jovi was about more than Jon's pretty face but to this day '7800...' is the record regarded by most people as the band's one flop.

For the rockers there was 'In And Out Of Love' and 'King Of The Mountain'. They still descended into bubble gum on occasion: 'Silent Night' was suffocatingly sentimental and 'Tokyo Road' (which drew on the band's experiences on their first tour of Japan where they had been an immediate hit) drearily romantic.

The critics drummed their fingers and conceded that the second Jovi album was certainly a more consistent recording than its predecessor. But compared to the other big attractions gobbling up the world's charts that year, '7800 Fahrenheit' seemed a modest achievement indeed. Van Halen had been on the road in America for nearly a year promoting their best-ever album, '1984'; Def Leppard had only recently broken records with their seven-million US break-through album, 'Pyromania'; meanwhile glam-metal kidz like Mötley Crüe and their less likeable imitators, Ratt, were hogging the hot spots in the US Top 10.

PolyGram had banked on '7800 Fahrenheit' propelling Bon Jovi into the same stratosphere. It didn't happen. The album failed to make the Top 40, struggling to equal the gold record they had received for 'Bon Jovi' (over 500,000 US sales). It was a bitter disappointment for the record company and they let Doc McGhee's office know they would have to go back to their ledgers and reconsider before bank-rolling another Bon Jovi album.

Displaying the same steely determination that would see him through all the peaks and troughs of his career, Jon elected to fight his corner and insisted he took the band out on the road anyway.

A support slot with Ratt was arranged. Ratt had achieved huge success in America in 1984 with their first full album, 'Out Of The Cellar', which sold over three million copies. But by the time 'Invasion Of Your Privacy', the follow-up, was issued a year later and Ratt set out for the first time as arena headliners, they were already in decline. Bon Jovi, on the other hand, had only temporarily stalled. And the crowd reaction

on that tour actually suggested the support act were getting a better response than the headliners. '7800...' might have failed to ignite the charts, but the band were more popular live on stage than ever. "It was all those years playing the bars and the dives," Jon mused afterwards. "Whatever you think of our latest record, put us on a stage somewhere, man, and we'll entertain you. Or die trying..."

Ratt, already insecure about their own talents and ever-fearful of being eclipsed by an opening act, imposed restrictions on Bon Jovi. Lack of soundchecks and a bare minimum of stage space were not exactly new disadvantages, but as Jon remarked, "Suddenly it was like we were in the way, like maybe we should leave. Just totally unfriendly. But all it did is make us even more determined to kick their ass every night!"

Relations with Ratt deteriorated, especially between Jon and the headliners' egocentric vocalist Stephen Pearcy, who had been particularly loathsome towards his support band. For a long time afterwards, to even mention his name in the same room as Jon was considered bad taste. How ironic that in 1993, Pearcy's new band Arcade (Ratt having split up) supported Bon Jovi on selected US dates.

"It was strange and funny having Stephen's band open for us," recalls Jon. "But I felt in no way a sense of triumph. It was just the way things go. Trouble is Stephen still can't work an audience that well!"

"We were just so rushed during that period," says Richie. "Rushed into making the second album, rushed into releasing it, and rushed into touring. The good part, I guess, was that it made us determined to make whatever came next something special."

" I love the idea of
cowboys roaming wherever
they choose. And I feel
that a modern rock band
is very much the same. "

WANTED: DEAD OR DEAD

" We could have written another 'Runaway'
in ten minutes, and if we had everybody would
have said it was a cop-out. "

Jon and the family: brother Anthony, father John Snr., Jon, mother Carol and brother Matt.

In July 1985, Bon Jovi were invited to participate in the high profile charity show, Farm Aid. It was conceived by John Cougar Mellencamp and country star Willie Nelson as an eloquent riposte to the enormously successful Live Aid. It aimed at raising funds for people in need on America's doorstep, farmers in the American mid-west region who were suffering cruel deprivations under the siege of Reagan economics.

Bon Jovi appeared on stage in Montana in the early hours of the morning, performing for just eight minutes in total, in front of some 83,000 fans, as well as millions more on TV. It was vital exposure for the band in their eventual national breakthrough, especially in the mid-west. They included a new song, 'Heart Of America', which was written virtually on the spot and offered a message as American as apple pie and drive-by shootings. It would become almost a cliché of the Bon Jovi back catalogue: never stop hoping, never stop dreaming, you-can-make-it-if-you-really-want-to. It was delicious. Jon Bon Jovi has always been a good flag-waver.

More proof that progress was being made, at least on the live front, followed soon after when Bon Jovi made a début headlining trek around the UK in May of 1985. They selected five venues – Manchester, Birmingham, London, Newcastle and Edinburgh – and sold them out, with Canadian chanteuse Lee Aaron in support. It was a tour that took the band to a new level in Britain.

Ipswich wasn't on the agenda, which everybody thought was a shame. During their first stay in the town, when the band had played there supporting Kiss, their entourage had 'entertained' two young female admirers back at the hotel in a manner that drew comparison with some of Led Zeppelin's alleged turpitude. Exactly what happened remains open to conjecture, but items of fruit and vegetables which were delivered on room service remained uneaten. Video evidence of the use to which the fruit and veg was put still exists, and the whole band (including JBJ) are caught on camera

enjoying the fun. Of course, this remains conjecture.

Back on a more professional footing, everyone who was there will certainly recall the band's appearance in London at the Dominion Theatre on May 23. I interviewed Jon the following morning, over breakfast by the side of a swimming pool. His parents had flown into England to see the show. Several record company heads had also been jetted in to see what was supposed to be the band's entrée into headliner status; Jon's first important step up the ladder since signing his record deal. And of course, every mildly curious musician in town without a gig of their own that night also made sure they were there.

It was do or die trying time... but things went awry when, after thundering through 'Tokyo Road', the opening number, the sound suddenly cut out as they entered into the riff for 'Get Ready'. Whether they had exceeded the decibel level of the venue's old-fashioned PA system, or whether they were the unfortunate victims of gremlins in the machinery, no-one at the time was sure. But where there had been noise and excitement, there was now only emptiness. Not even the vocal mikes worked. It lasted only a short time before the sound came back, and Richie carried on with his solo – and then the sound system gave out again! As the roadies desperately scurried about in the worried side-stage shadows, Jon briefly left the stage. Returning with a 12-string guitar and that "I don't know any jokes, sorry," he proceeded to conduct... a singalong.

Here was a man facing one of the most crucial gigs of his career (headlining in a city regarded as being among the three principle seats of influence in the music world, the others being New York and Los Angeles) and the machines have chosen just that moment to start fighting back! A lesser performer might have crumbled, but Jon won over the capacity crowd with his bravura, and so successful was his singalong that when the sound system buzzed back to life, he turned around and said: "No, I don't want the fucking PA!" He took things a little further, continuing with his strumming, before being coaxed back into 'Roulette' by the rest of the band. If he had engineered and stage-managed the whole thing, Jon couldn't have done his reputation any more good. It was sheer genius. It also persuaded many of the industry big-wigs that they were dealing with someone rather special.

The next morning he was very matter of fact about it. "When the PA blew up... we just laughed at it. We didn't get pissed off or walk off and throw tantrums. I pulled out the acoustic and began joking around, you know, what else can I do?"

I asked the then recently turned 23 year old where he saw his life going.

"I don't know about that." He shook the fluffy bouffant hair that stood as tall as a wig. "I only know about the music, at this point. Where I'm coming from is the same place as all the people I listen to, the Tom Pettys and the U2s, Little Steven, The Babys... you know, lyrically, you gotta be saying something in your songs. I think we've sacrificed commerciality a little bit in an effort to achieve those aims.

"We could have written another 'Runaway' in about 10 minutes, and if we had everybody would have said it was just a cop-out. I couldn't do that, I need to see some growth here myself."

As a result of the success of the UK tour, he was offered an appearance at Donington on August 17, 1985, third on a bill topped by ZZ Top, then enjoying enormous success with their synth-boogie 'Eliminator' album and attendant hit singles. Special guests were the British progressive band Marillion. Below the Jovis were the fast-rising thrash heroes Metallica, Ratt (in Europe, even at their height, the LA rodents could never compete with Bon Jovi) and homespun English cult rockers Magnum. It was a precariously balanced bill, but Bon Jovi were the surprise of the day... though their performance did get off to a somewhat disturbing start when someone at the front of the crowd actually heaved a severed pig's head onto the stage! "It was totally, but totally gross," he winced afterwards. "I mean, what do you say to something like that?" Who knew what it meant? Jon wisely decided to take it as a thumbs-up and proceeded to tear up the stage.

Jon was confident that the band would return to Donington one day and headline. "We'll make it, just you wait and see!" he promised. Whether his confidence was truly heartfelt, or just putting on his usual brave face for the media, who could tell – but back they came in 1987. And this time they were headlining.By the end of 1985, however, Bon Jovi hadn't achieved the big breakthrough so many had predicted. But they had moved a little further up the curve. '7800 Degrees Fahrenheit' took the band beyond a million units world-wide, which was a very healthy base. And in certain key parts of the globe they were performing their own shows to increasingly receptive audiences.

But the pressure was on. In the cut and thrust atmosphere of the Eighties, major labels were unwilling to bankroll bands who failed to succeed on a superstar level after three albums, an absurd deadline and one which invariably resulted in acts being either pressured too soon or falling at the last hurdle. In the long term, as the history of rock attests, those bands which have been allowed to progress naturally are the ones who sustain their careers the longest. But with the major labels now coming increasingly under the ownership of corporate business structures – as opposed to experienced music men – the bottom line was all that mattered, and Bon Jovi had to deliver third time out – or else. In fact, persistent rumours suggested that the band were into their ninth life as far as Polygram was concerned. Derek Shulman has always denied it but there is no doubt that Bon Jovi were in serious danger of being dropped.

British music entrepreneur Jonathan King, who was retained on a consultancy basis by the London-based wing of the company, told the author in Moscow that he issued a memo pointing out that although Bon Jovi's live performance fan-base appeared to lie in the same long-haired heavy metal fans they had been playing to on other bands' bills for the last two years, their true appeal as recording artists lay in a much more pragmatic, chart-friendly direction.

"Bon Jovi has never been an out-and-out heavy metal band," King pointed out. "Basically, they're a pop band. Bon Jovi are pop dressed as metal. And I felt that point was being missed by some of the higher-ups at the company who couldn't understand why they weren't becoming a huge metal band like AC/DC or someone like that. I pointed out that where their success really lay was not with long-haired boys, but long-haired girls..."

After Bon Jovi had gone super-nova, King ran into the band on a Concorde flight from New York to London, and Jon took the time to thank him personally for the helping hand.

But what Bon Jovi patently needed at this juncture was a radical rethink in the studio. They needed hit singles to boost their sales potential into the multi-millions. Either that, or face the axe. The first move was to dispose of Lance Quinn. Nobody was exactly happy with his contribution on '7800...', so even if the pressure hadn't been exerted from on high, the chances are that he would have gone anyway. The second album had been a horrible experience all round for the band; they needed a clean break.

WANTED: DEAD OR DEAD

WANTED: DEAD OR DEAD

In came Canadian Bruce Fairbairn, and a move from the relatively cloistered Warehouse Studios to the more cosmopolitan climes of Little Mountain Studios in Vancouver. Of course, with hindsight it seems a stroke of genius to work with someone of Fairbairn's stature, but at the time he first met Bon Jovi the quietly-spoken Canadian was far from being a major name. He had gained success through Loverboy, Blue Öyster Cult, Honeymoon Suite, and Black 'N Blue, all of whom had provided the producer with hits, if not quite on the scale he was about to encounter with Bon Jovi. Plus, he was known for bringing projects in under budget, an important consideration given the perilous state of the band's finances.

Fairbairn brought an extra dimension to Bon Jovi. In addition, Desmond Child was brought in as a co-writer for the first time. A relative unknown, he had gained cult status among aficionados of melodic rock thanks to his otherwise obscure Desmond Child & Rouge outfit. He airbrushed some of the rougher edges out of the Bon Jovi songwriting technique, and though his reputation was far from made, there is no doubt that it was his contribution that was most significant to the eventual success of the third Bon Jovi album – though Jon will probably go to his grave denying it.

"There are those who believe that Desmond played an important part in breaking Bon Jovi," Jon complained to a recent biographer. "But they forget that at the time we worked with him for the first time, he wasn't that established. In all honesty, we helped him as much as he helped us."

Jon took up residence at a rented apartment on the New Jersey shoreline with girlfriend (and future wife) Dorothea Hurley during the weeks preceding the album's release, and the band used this as a base to do a promotional round of interviews and photo shoots. There was an air of confident optimism about the five-piece as they prepared for the task ahead. Away from the pressures of the metropolis, Jon in particular seemed relaxed and primed. The album was done, dusted and ready on the launchpad, and there was a certain feeling that the moment of truth had arrived for them. Certainly, the air of nonchalance surrounding Bon Jovi seemed real enough.

In truth, while there was talk of hit singles and a big album, nobody was prepared for what was going to happen next. 'Slippery When Wet' was released in August of 1986, and was to spend a total of 15 weeks in two bursts at the top of the US charts. It peaked at No. 6 in the UK, and went on to sell in excess of 18 million copies world-wide. It became one of the biggest-selling records of the Eighties and although they may have still been little more than another 'scarves and make-up' heavy metal band to the critics, with 'Slippery...' Bon Jovi achieved something previously thought impossible for a heavy metal band: credibility with teenage girls. Simultaneously, the album did much to re-establish album-oriented long-haired rock as a commercial force in the pop mainstream.

'You Give Love A Bad Name' was the first single from the album. It had instant commercial appeal and reached No. 14 in the UK. But in the States it roared through to the top of the charts. Jon heard about 'You Give Love...' while on a pay-phone backstage at .38 Special show, jumping up and down, unable to believe it. Vindication was his – he'd arrived. There was no stopping him now.

Bon Jovi had elected to begin their tour work on the 'Slippery...' trek supporting Southern rockers .38 Special in arenas across the US. It was perceived as no more than a warm-up – and a fail-safe. Should 'Slippery...' not have happened, then Bon Jovi were not committed to a costly headline tour of their own. It was a shrewd tactic, but ultimately unnecessary. It soon became obvious who was selling tickets, and who was along for the ride!

Of course, it hadn't all been smooth sailing with the album. The original design for that sleeve featured a close-up shot of the chest of a well-endowed young lady, barely covered by a skimpy T-shirt bearing the legend 'Slippery When Wet'. The design was to prove just a little too risqué for most markets, and this sleeve appeared only in Japan. The cover that adorned 'Slippery...' in most territories was far less distracting, featuring the title scrawled on a black plastic bag covered with water.

Before 'Slippery...' was released, Jon had came up with a master stroke. He took the tapes containing all the songs down to a local pizza parlour in New Jersey..." We just got in a load of kids hanging around, let them listen to the songs and let them choose which ones they felt worked best. After all, these are the sort of people whom we are making the record for, so why not let them choose for themselves?"

PolyGram believed in it sufficiently to sanction a huge marketing push, and there was no doubting the radio-friendliness of singles like 'You Give Love A Bad Name' and 'Livin' On A Prayer'. Desmond Child had given the band a lighter touch compared to previous albums, and Fairbairn's production gave the record a contemporary sound.

More significantly than that, perhaps, 'Slippery...' perfectly captured the Eighties: this was Reaganomic rock at its apotheosis, big shoulders, bigger hair, and the shrill voice of expectancy wailing like a siren through the streets of your heart. It was even nicely packaged. Jonathan King's 'pop-dressed-as-metal' prognosis had been remarkably accurate.

RAW magazine in the UK rated it as one of the crucial releases of the Eighties. Trevor White, producer at Capital Radio, now a senior executive with Virgin Radio, called it "the template of the perfect rock album. They'll never make a more perfect album than they did with 'Slippery When Wet'. It's impossible. But that's all right, because none of their contem poraries like Aerosmith or Def Leppard are going to make a better album than 'Slippery...'. One of the classic albums of all time, without a doubt."

And the rapidity with which radio stations across the globe picked up on the music underlined the potency of the band's burgeoning mainstream appeal. 'You Give Love...', the first hit off 'Slippery...', was aimed at one of Jon's former girlfriends, actress Diane Lane. The only famous girl Jon had ever dated, the pair met backstage at a show at Madison Square Garden in New York. Now, this was before the big Bon breakthrough, so Diane (star of *The Cotton Club* among other movies) was the celebrity. And in a state of inebriation, it was she who picked up Jon, not vice versa.

Their relationship was short, sharp and not-so-sweet, hence the inspiration for 'You Give Love...'. 'Livin' On A Prayer', though, has a blue-collar atmo- sphere that recalls Bruce Springsteen, with Jon waxing cod-philosophical about the struggle facing working class America in Reagan's 'brave new world'..."I write what I feel," he says. And what he felt was the touch of someone in sync with the American heartbeat. The other stand-out track was 'Wanted: Dead Or Alive', a hugely popular live attraction, which features a world-weary Jon singing about life on the road, the oldest cliché in the book, but somehow he made it sound fresh and interesting again, if, as always, there was a little romantic marmalade; Jon's fascina- tion with cowboys going into overdrive as he croons about the 'steel horse' he rides. "I love the idea of cow- boys roaming wherever they choose. And I feel that a modern rock band is very much the same. We do ride into town for a brief time, play our show before moving on to the next town."

Bon Jovi's official biographer Malcolm Dome reckons that this song has "a certain relationship to the mighty Westerns of the great film director John Ford, but also draws from the nihilist homilies of Sergei Leone and *Shane*, self-reliant, lone-riding icons of freedom and justice. The lyrical charm of 'Wanted...' is that it does possess a desperate edge. The glories of being in a rock band on tour are balanced against the tedium and the pain."

Jon's sex appeal was obviously the other main ingredient behind their sudden success. Naturally photogenic, he exuded a wholesome, matinée idol appeal that made him a hit with women of all ages. There was nothing threatening about his clean-cut image. Boys identified; girls fantasised. Exhibiting none of the self-destructive wilfulness of a James Dean, or, latterly, an Axl Rose, there was a charm and innocence to Jon's appeal. It meant that he could appear as comfortably in the pages of *Smash Hits* as in *Kerrang!*

Nobody could dispute that by the end of 1986, Jon Bon Jovi was *the* rock star pin-up. This presence and position was also underlined by some expertly wrought promotional videos, designed to show off the band's hugely ambitious live arena-filling presentation to the maximum extent. As with Michael Jackson's 'Thriller', Prince's 'Purple Rain', and Guns n' Roses' 'Appetite For Destruction', 'Slippery When Wet' was a hugely successful artistic statement that wound its way into the very social fabric of the era it mirrored. If you wanna know about 1986, just slap on this record. It says it all.

Jon and wife Dorothea.

Dave Sabo:
❝ He's for real in some way I don't think I've met in anybody else in this stupid business ❞

❝ I can't believe how sick I look. White as a ghost with big black circles under my eyes. It's frightening. ❞

❝ If people come up to me and are real nice, I'll do anything ❞

SLIPPERY

Fame affects different people in different ways. Some are driven into a hole in the ground in a desperate attempt to find the seclusion they have sacrificed. Others become publicity junkies whose ugly faces constantly scan the media for a mention, or zap onto MTV to check they're rotating the video.

Apart from those first few holding-on-for-dear-life early months, Jon Bon Jovi has somehow managed to maintain as balanced a perspective on mega-fame and how to deal with it, as any superstar anywhere. But then, he learned the hard way. He's not a controversial character by nature. He doesn't trash hotel rooms, and declines to hop between the sheets with every girl who offers herself. Just about the only girlfriend he has ever had who could be called a 'celebrity' was the actress Diane Lane. "If people come up to me and are real nice, I'll do anything - take pictures, sign autographs," said Jon around the time of 'Slippery...'. "The way I look at it, these are the people who have put me up where I am today. They have bought the albums and concert tickets. Without them, where would Bon Jovi be?"

After 'Slippery...' things went through the roof, with especially obsessive fans camping outside his home in New Jersey. "That was crazy. Now, it's died down quite a lot. There are always one or two fans hanging around outside. But so long as they don't cross the threshold and try to enter the house, then it doesn't bother me. In fact, I usually send somebody out from the house to make sure they are OK."

At the end of 1986, the band sold out 14 shows in the UK, beginning on November 7 at Bradford St. George's Hall ending with their last of four dates at London's Hammersmith Odeon, on November 25. To celebrate the enormous success, Phonogram Records in the UK held a party for them at Break For The Border, a Mexican

The Bon Jovi family home.

restaurant in London's West End. After an hour, the sound-system, which had been blasting out various rock bands signed to the label, was suddenly turned up several notches for 'You Give Love A Bad Name'. Right on cue the band made their entrance, surrounded by Phonogram personnel. The embarrassment on Jon's face was obvious.

Even the old Sayreville house in New Jersey became famous during the 'Slippery When Wet' period when it was bought by MTV, who gave it away in one of their more tasteless on-air competitions. Any outrage in the Jovi camp at this invasion of their privacy was forgotten when the influential TV station rotated their videos in ever increasing numbers.

"I missed the last eight months of the 'Slippery When Wet' tour because I was just totally physically and mentally blitzed," Richie told me when it was all over. "But then, after I thought about it, it's still the biggest thing that ever happened to me. A real once-in-a-lifetime thing.

"But the responsibility of playing all over the world in so many places where we'd never even been before, just touring and touring our asses off, it nearly killed us, man. Trying to have some fun at the same time as all that shit was going on nearly drove me crazy."

One aspect of fame was that people would now take Jon's opinions on almost any subject very seriously indeed, especially when it concerned an offer to personally become involved in helping another band's career, as happened in the case of the previously unknown Philadelphia band Cinderella.

Jon used his influence to good effect, getting Cinderella a recording contract with PolyGram. "I saw Cinderella play at a club in Philadelphia and was really impressed with what I saw," Jon recalled. "Their vocalist, Tom Keifer, was particularly strong. So I persuaded Derek Shulman to go down and have a look at them." The result was a record deal followed by much exposure, courtesy of Bon Jovi, both in terms of constant plugs in magazines and crucial slots at key Bon Jovi shows.

"I got help from people like Southside Johnny when I was starting out – and I was always grateful to them for that help. Now I am in a position to aid others, I would be neglecting my beliefs if I didn't do what I can for them."

The other band which Bon Jovi helped to find considerable success was fellow New Jersey residents Skid Row, whose guitarist was Dave 'Snake' Sabo, Jon's old friend from school and The Wild Ones. "We had always kind of said, you know, which ever one makes it first, he'll come back and help out the other," Dave told me. "Jon's a really good guy like that. He never forgets a fuckin' thing, man. He's for real in some way I don't think I've met yet in anybody else in this stupid business."

Jon constantly pushed Skid Row in interviews, urging Doc McGhee to sign the band for management, which McGhee duly did, and they signed with Atlantic Records. When the first, self-titled Skid Row album was released in 1989, Jon gave them a further boost by taking them out on the road as 'special guests' on the next Bon Jovi world tour.

Jon and the band spent 1986 and 1987 touring, traversing the world more than once, setting new attendance records at many venues. It was a trek that in hindsight proved way too long and laborious.

The climax came in the UK on August 22, 1987, when Bon Jovi headlined at the prestigious Castle Donington Monsters Of Rock Festival. By the mid-Eighties, Donington had become the premier global event for rockers. Certainly, the invitation to headline was a much coveted accolade, a dream and a promise come true for Jon. It was also significant in that whatever their chart and pop success, they were still regarded as essentially a rock band.

"It's the kids who've broken this band without a doubt," Jon told *Kerrang!*."We really have come through the traditional ways. We're not an overnight sensation, we're a hard-working band with over 500 shows under our belts. It's always been a very honest thing, and people have responded to that."

Contrast this with what had happened two years earlier with ZZ Top who, amazingly, had earned the displeasure of rock fans because they'd got daytime radio air play!

Nevertheless, the promoters were taking no chances and the rest of the bill at Donington 1987 was decidedly heavy. Joining Bon Jovi on the bill were special guests Dio (fronted by former Rainbow/Black Sabbath singer Ronnie James Dio), Metallica (like the Jovis, and indeed Dio, making their second trip to the festival), Anthrax (New York thrashers), W.A.S.P. (LA schlock rockers) and Cinderella (Jon's good deed). The bill attracted more than 70,000 fans to the site

The denim 'n' leather all-male brigade had been the bastion of the festival's support up until that point, but Bon Jovi's chart profile meant that a number of girls turned up for the show. Amusement and horror were registered in equal measure (depending on your viewpoint) when those clearly new to festival requirements came dressed for a fashion show.

Inevitably the heavens opened during the morning and Donington's open air grass auditorium was turned into an unholy mud bath. Fortunately, the rain stopped just before Cinderella took to the stage at 1.00pm, but the damage had been done – and much of the festival's bonhomie ruined.

Bon Jovi made their arrival at the site in cars during the late afternoon, while helicopters flew overhead, acting as decoys for any fans waiting in ambush. On arrival, the band were quickly ushered into their own enclosure, where security was strict. Not everyone was enamoured of the decoy chopper idea. The helicopters thrummed over the site during Metallica's set, effectively sabotaging the Californian thrashers in mid-whirl. They were not amused, accusing Jon of doing it deliberately, a charge he's always denied. Yet, Jon must have known the timing for each band on the bill. So, why choose to 'arrive' by chopper just when Metallica were getting into their stride?

Backstage, Jon seemed tired. The usual sparkle was missing from his eyes and his voice trailed off listlessly. He invited the author into his trailer for half-an-hour while he was getting ready. Heavily bearded, with deep black patches beneath both eyes, he seemed pumped up but brittle; this wasn't stage

**Jon on stage during the
'Slippery When Wet' tour.**

nerves, though, this was real tension, deep exhaustion.
He eyed me fiercely. "Even you," he said, "when I just
invite you in here to say hello, you pull a tape-recorder
out and start asking me to do things..."

"Oh man, by Donington I was so shot up with
steroids and anything else the doctor could give me to
keep me working, I was a wreck," he explained to me
some time later. "I didn't know it at the time, but I was
gone, fucked, done. Don't forget, that was 14 months
into the tour, with another three to go before we finished,
and the pressure was on...

"I've got some amazing pictures that were taken
from that stage of the tour. There was one in particular
of me and Little Steven together somewhere, and man,
I look so wasted. I can't believe how sick I look!
White as a ghost with big black circles under my eyes.
It's frightening..."

How much Jon was enjoying the success of the
band towards the end of the 'Slippery...' world tour
remains open to debate. But Donington was certainly
the climax. Indeed, the band gave their all in another
fine performance, even if the opening didn't exactly go
as planned. Jon was supposed to slide down a rope onto
the centre of the stage as the band burst into life – the
super-hero's entry. The trick worked, but hardly anyone
realised it had taken place – for the spotlight failed to
pick out Jon on his descent stagewards. Once into their
stride, however, the band gave a memorable performance
worthy of the occasion and their status as headliners.

And at encore time, Bon Jovi dragged on Twisted
Sister vocalist Dee Snider, Paul Stanley from Kiss and
Iron Maiden's Bruce Dickinson to fulfil yet another
tradition of the Jovi tour. "We always invite people up
for the encore. It's not a whole big deal. We just enjoy
it," Jon explained a year later.

"At Donington, we asked Metallica to come up for the
encore, but I heard they were all pissed off at me because
we flew over in the helicopter during their set. I mean,
I had no idea that happened until somebody told me
later, so I apologised, but it wasn't an intentional thing,
you know. That was just when we happened to be arriving.

"I also asked Ronnie Dio if he wanted to come up,
but he said no. But Paul Stanley and Dee Snider and
Bruce Dickinson all got up. Anyone who's there, that
was the theme of last year's tour. If you're here, you
gotta work, too. Because that's the way it is around
here. And the kids, I think, enjoy that. They liked that
kind of camaraderie on stage."

Bon Jovi were to tour for another three months,
using the private jet they had been flying in since
'Slippery...' broke them into the big time. In all, they
had toured for some 16 months, played a total of more
than 130 shows, accruing a gross income of over $28
million. In the process, 'Slippery...' had gone on to
touch nearly 18 million sales world-wide, and by the
end of '87, it was official: 'Slippery...' was the biggest
selling hard rock album of all time.

So, what next? For most it would have meant a
break in which to catch breath, enjoy their status and
plan ahead. But, much to the surprise of everybody, Jon
elected to jump straight into the recording of album
number four. It was, with hindsight, a mistake.

" New Jersey is not a place, it's an attitude. **"**

" Most bands are fortunate if the kind of success we had with 'Slippery...' happens to them once in their career. **"**

JERSEY SYNDICATE

Jon in Slash mode.

Bon Jovi returned to work after just a six week break. The band groaned inwardly and gritted their teeth, but Jon was intent on making the most of their new-found status. "We just felt strong enough and good enough to get back into the writing groove," says Jon. "Richie came over to my place every day and we sat in my bedroom and just wrote. In fact, by Christmas 1987 we had about 17 songs already demoed and ready to go."

The band went into full rehearsal, where another dozen songs were co-written by Jon and Richie. The original idea had been to do a double album, a bold move, but one that Jon himself felt strongly about, but at the eleventh hour, after much tough-talking behind closed doors, it was decided to abandon the idea and go for a single. Though a double-album might have satisfied Jon's desire for artistic credibility to go with his multi-platinum sales, it would almost certainly be at the cost of those same multi-sqillion sales.

"The little girls don't buy double-albums," scoffed a former PolyGram exec. "You're onto a good thing if you can persuade them to buy your singles, let alone confuse everybody by expecting mum or dad to cough up the extra for a double-album."

Recording again took place in Vancouver with Bruce Fairbairn at the controls. "Why fix what ain't broke, that was the basic philosophy behind the album," Jon told me when we met in Dublin on the eve of the band's first show of the 'New Jersey' world tour. As ever, though, he would always get hot under the collar at any suggestion that he had somehow discovered a hidden formula for success.

Originally, the band had intended calling the record 'Sons Of Beaches'; they even went so far as to mock up a sleeve for the album, based on The Doors'

'Strange Days' album: a montage set on the Jersey shoreline, with the band alongside a number of fascinatingly grotesque characters. It was the second time Bon Jovi were forced to scrap an album cover. At McGhee's insistence, and under pressure from the suits at PolyGram, 'Sons Of Beaches' metamorphosed into 'New Jersey'. The idea came to Jon from a patch he wore on his jacket during the 'Slippery...' tour.

"New Jersey is not a place, it's an attitude," Jon told *RAW*. "The attitude can be found in any town, wherever you're from. We're good buddies with Def Leppard and they've got that same outlook. They dig where they come from, they know what they do for a living, and they enjoy it, and that's the kind of approach you've got to have, no matter what your profession is, no matter whether you're from New Jersey or Iowa or Sheffield."

Determined to stay as close to their roots as possible, Jon again opted to let his peers choose the track listing for him. This time Bruce Fairbairn's baby-sitters were placed in the A&R hot-seat for a night. Bringing with them some of their friends, who also pulled in some kids who were hanging around the studio, the whole gang sat and listened while the fresh 'New Jersey' tapes rolled...

"Some were fans, others hated us and there were a few who couldn't give a damn," Jon recalled with a smile. He simply sat them down, played the album and then heard the opinions. What the kids chose was a selection of songs as strong and chart-ready as anything the band had done.

'New Jersey' was a surprisingly positive-sounding collection. If there was a sense of anxiety or tiredness about the band, it certainly didn't show up on the final product. 'Stick To Your Guns' and 'Wild Is The Wind' were originally going to be saved for the next album, (they had suffered in the sudden revisions that were required following the decision to discard the double-album idea). But several of the kids who had been brought in to listen to the songs picked up specifically on those two, and Jon picked up on their enthusiasm immediately.

"We were scared shitless," he admitted at the time. The record opened with the tribal thud of 'Lay Your Hands On Me'. 'Bad Medicine', the first single to be released from 'New Jersey', followed, and the accompanying video was also a departure. Once again, the band put their trust in the fans, giving out 150 video cameras to the lucky ones invited along to the video shoot – and getting them to film the clip! This was then mixed with live concert footage shot by a professional crew. Moreover, the band played a 90-minute free show – their first live date of 1988 – for those fans who came along to the video shoot, as a way of paying them back for patiently sitting through endless lip-synched takes.

Back in 'New Jersey' territory, the song 'Blood On Blood' was very much a family affair. Bon Jovi have always seen themselves as a close-knit family, with everything that entails, including arguments, major bust-ups, but always the loyalty and bond of 'belonging'. This was, perhaps, the first time those emotions had been so eloquently expressed in song (though it takes its name from a phrase used repeatedly in 'Highway Patrolman', a narrative ballad with similar themes on Bruce Springsteen's 1982 'Nebraska' album). 'Ride Cowboy Ride' again locked into Jon's fascination with the Western themes so brilliantly espoused on 'Wanted: Dead Or Alive', and 'I'll Be There For You' was a big-haired ballad and another world-wide hit.

"In a way, what I wanted was to feel the high we attained with 'Slippery...' all over again," says Jon. "But with hindsight we didn't have enough time between albums. It did burn us out. I remember being in Dublin at the RDS Hall (on October 31 1988 - the start of the world tour)... I came in when Lita Ford was on stage, and I like her a lot, it was me who picked her for the tour. But I just thought, 'Get her the fuck off the stage! I'm here, there's kids here, I want to go to work!'

"I was just so nuts, I wanted to get up there with her and grab the microphone... I was on fucking fire!"

"It's funny, some MTV guys were there – they're doing an around–the–world–with–Bon Jovi type of thing – and one of them said to me, 'What do you want to tell the folks back in America?' I said, 'Get ready motherfuckers, I'm BACK!'

"Honestly, man, I had so much adrenaline running through me last night everybody must have thought I was just loaded. You know, totally wired for sound. And Lita's up there singing, 'Kiss me once...'. And I'm thinking, 'Yeah, yeah, get the fuck off the stage! I'm in a hurry!' I was like the beast unchained..."

The Bon Jovi 'New Jersey' tour opened up in Europe, trekking its way through Dublin (where Joe Elliot joined them for the encore rendering of 'The Boys Are Back In Town'), before heading to the mainland and dates in Glasgow, Birmingham, London. Four sold-out shows at Wembley Arena proved that they were no longer a phenomenon, but a well-established rock band.

The fear of following up the success of 'Slippery...', though, was clearly evident in the band's attitude and approach. The record came out in October of 1988 and hit the top slot on both sides of the Atlantic. 'New Jersey' went some way further to proving that Bon Jovi was more than just another pop group.

Given the exhaustion factor after the 'Slippery...' tour, surely this time around things would be rather pared down? Not so, Jon told me in Dublin: "You know I keep hearing that too, but every time I confront Doc McGhee with it he kind of mumbles something under his breath and leaves the room. But I know it's scheduled to go right the way through '89.

"Where things go from there, we'll have to see how the record's done and how we're holding before we make a definite decision. We're going to hit a lot of uncharted ground on this tour, though. We're gonna go to South America, hopefully, and a bunch of other places we've never had a chance to go to before."

But was it necessary to get back on the road so quickly with a new album to keep up momentum?

"I don't think so, not at this point. It just seemed to be the right time, we felt we had the songs. I felt that the songs were as good as I could ask for at that given time, you know, without spending four years writing an album, or whatever..."

"Most bands are fortunate if the kind of success we had with 'Slippery...' happens to them once in their career. And hardly anybody ever matches the success they had the first time an album really took off for them.

"This was the thing that was driving me crazy before we sat down to write the new songs. I'm thinking, 'How do you follow something like that? Michael Jackson didn't do it. Billy Idol didn't do it. Billy Joel didn't do it. Springsteen, Prince, Madonna... How the hell are we gonna do it if those guys didn't?' I was driving myself crazy with this shit! And I wanted it to happen again. Sure I did! Not for monetary reasons, either. But because, man, when you can go out and headline at major places like Donington, that's a major thrill... to walk out there on stage and go 'Hi' and 70,000 kids go 'Hi!' right back. You just think, 'Holy shit, this is unreal! Gimme more!'

"On the home stretch of the last tour we did three nights at Madison Square Garden, three at Meadowlands and three at Nassau Coliseum. When you do something like that, you just don't ever want to do less again. I want to be able to do things like that on every tour. And the thing is, when things started going crazy on the last tour, it was the first time around for us... Things were happening so fast, we didn't have time to think about what we were doing, we just did it.

"It wasn't until it was all over that we realised what we had done. And then we really needed to do it again. We wanted to prove to ourselves that this wasn't just a one–off. We saw the whole thing as a big challenge.

"On 'New Jersey' I also think we've grown up as writers. That's probably the best way for me to put it. I think Richie and I have moved on quite a bit from where we started. But it's like anything, the more you practise, the better you get at it. At the same time, I don't think we're ever gonna write songs that are as involved, let's say, socially or politically, or what have you, as, say, someone like U2. Because to me that's not what we're about.

"I've read a hundred times over the years in magazines that we write these clichéd adolescent lyrics about friendship. And I think, 'Shit, friendship's always been pretty important to me, maybe even more important in a kid's life'. And these social issues people talk about... I know when I was 16 or 17 years old I was more worried about getting a car, getting laid and making my first buck than I was about who was gonna be the next President of the United States, you know?

"And maybe that sounds a little self–indulgent, but on the other hand it's true! That's a lot of what growing up as a teenager in America is all about. And that's what I write about in my songs, because that's what I experienced. I've never run for President..."

But beyond the fact that the material was more 'grown up', Jon's voice had also changed... for the better.

"I think it keeps getting better with each album. I prefer my voice now to the sound of it on any of the other albums. Also, from the end of the last tour through to this year, I've gone back to taking lessons. And it's really paid off. I mean, I know last night my voice was in real good shape, and I'd pay millions to keep it that way every night.

"That's why psychologically I needed last night to be a good night for me with all my heart. I needed to come out and sing great, but I know that I could also come out and sing great again tonight. I can't burn it any more, I want all this to still mean something to me when I wake up the next day."

Of course, there was a certain luxury to travel now that they had the use of a private plane, as Jon explained to me in Dublin:

"Yeah, we're gonna be travelling that way when we get back to America, too. It's the same one Def Leppard were using for the last leg of their tour over there. They had their logo, 'Hystouria', real little up front. We're having it repainted right now with the words 'The Jersey Syndicate'. That's what all the backstage passes say, too. This isn't the Bon Jovi tour. It's the Jersey Syndicate tour..."

And Jon still found time to share a good night out on occasion with old friends, such as Joe Elliot... "Oh man, we were both so bombed one night, I can hardly remember... I think we ran into each other in Vancouver and I really pulled a number on him. He wanted to go out to a club and I said, 'No, you've become too boring since you stopped drinking. I ain't going out unless you agree to have a drink with me, you know?'

"But Joe said OK, and we went out for what was supposed to be a quiet drink together... Only one drink led to another, like these things have a tendency to do, and I kept filling his glass and he kept filling mine, until we were both completely rat-assed! We ended up getting on stage at this tiny club somewhere in the city – us and Dan Reed and this chick from The Headpins (Darby Mills) – and we're all trying to play 'Rock And Roll' by Led Zeppelin, and none of us can even stand up! We were all over the place! We had to be helped off the stage before people started throwing things...

"Joe told me that he hasn't had a drink since, although I can tell you he poured himself a Scotch in our dressing room before the gig last night. Which pretty much started the night for both of us."

The 'New Jersey' tour alone amounted to 237 shows in just 16 months, an incredible work-rate that few bands would even attempt. They had finally succeeded in headlining at Giants Stadium in New Jersey (home of Jon's beloved American football team, The New York Giants), which was the realisation of another dream come true, and they had returned to the UK to play at Milton Keynes Bowl alongside Europe, Skid Row and Vixen.

Jon came back down to earth in March when he was arrested after staggering onto the Wollman Ice Skating Rink in New York's Central Park at 3.30 am. He was picked up for trespassing with girlfriend Dorothea Hurler and a couple of people from the McGhee office. It was all harmless fun, but it made the front page news, such was Jon's celebrity status. That very same month, ironically, the Mayor of New York declared a Bon Jovi Day in honour of what the band had achieved, and in the process gave them the keys to the city!

And Jon finally married long-time sweetheart Dorothea on April 29, 1989, at the Graceland Chapel in Las Vegas. Jon was also planning a huge US extravaganza in the summer. "We're talking about doing stadium shows now. Maybe for the beginning of the Summer. At the moment, the idea is that us, Mötley Crüe and Skid Row would be a good weekend package. I'd love to do that, it would be so cool to pull that one off...

Would you be headlining?

"Of course we would be fucking headlining!"

But come the Summer, there was that Milton Keynes show to play. Jon had contemplated trying to play at Wembley Stadium instead of Milton Keynes, but Bros (huge stars in Britain that year, largely forgotten the next) were already booked into the weekend slot – August 18 – Bon Jovi wanted. Thus, unable to repeat themselves by going back to Donington – there was no Donington that year because two fans had died tragically on the site, asphyxiated in the mud as the crowd surged towards the front of the stage during a set by Guns N' Roses the previous year – Milton Keynes Bowl seemed the perfect halfway house. The band helicoptered in from London. "We passed over Wembley Stadium on the way," Jon later remembered, "and there were not a lot of people there. It was gratifying to know that even up against one of the trendiest of chart bands we could still prove to be a better crowd puller!"

At the time I was presenting a weekly show on London's Capital Radio, who were one of the main sponsors of the festival, and I was asked to help compère the Milton Keynes show. As a result, I was fortunate enough to watch the entire show from the side of the stage, and with Aerosmith singer Steven Tyler and guitarist Joe Perry joining the Jovis for a run-through of Aerosmiths classic 'Walk This Way' at encore time, there was a truly festive atmosphere.

But amidst the joy shadows lurked. There were some strange rumours circulating that Jon had threatened both Tico and Alec with the sack unless they lost some excess body fat – and that the pair had been despatched to undergo lipo-suction. Jon denies this allegation and also the fact that Bon Jovi had ceased to be a band and had become his own personal property, but the stories persisted.

Other storm clouds were gathering, and the next couple of years, although augmenting the band's success, also brought trauma. It began with the arrest of manager Doc McGhee on charges of drug smuggling, and continued with amazing allegations from Skid Row. The hitherto tranquil existence of the New Jersey Syndicate was to be threatened on several levels, bringing a whole new meaning to Jon's statement that: "I run things like the Memphis Mafia" (a reference to Elvis Presley's notorious entourage).

However, all seemed tranquil enough when Bon Jovi ended the year with a special charity show at London's Hammersmith Odeon, all proceeds going to the Nordoff-Robbins Foundation, which aims to help handicapped children through music. In what was primarily an acoustic evening, the band were joined on stage by none other than Jimmy Page... and Bon Jovi seemed in no way overawed by his presence, a measure of just how far they'd come.

Bon Jovi with their private jet.

7

" At this stage of the game, it's like you ask yourself what can we do that Zeppelin or The Stones or The Beatles didn't do already... "

BAD MEDICINE

" I see alot of kids in my travels. Most of them don't know what they're doing with their lives. "

" When I was very young, I used to do a lot of drugs. "

Jon in Russia.

Doc McGhee was placed under formal arrest in April 1988, charged with drug smuggling, specifically, playing a key role in an attempt six years earlier to smuggle more than 40,000 lbs of cannabis from Colombia into North Carolina. Only a few eyebrows were raised in the US music industry. "Everybody knew Doc had a past," claims one former associate who wishes to remain anonymous. "But as long as he was making plenty of money for everybody, who cared? It wasn't until he got busted that everybody suddenly got all self-righteous about it."

With his ample girth and non-stop verbiage, McGhee was a flamboyant personality in an increasingly corporate-minded industry that lacked such figures. He was a throwback to the days when a rock manager led his troops by example, smashing up hotel rooms and indulging in exotic brain-tranquillisers with the best of 'em, an echo reaching back to the long-gone days when legendary killer-managers like Don Arden (ELO), Peter Grant (Led Zeppelin), Chas Chandler (Jimi Hendrix & Slade), and Malcolm MacLaren (Sex Pistols) ruled the rock world.

From the Irish ghettos of New York, McGhee had come to the record business first as a promoter of local college shows, then more seriously as a manager of Canadian singer/guitarist Pat Travers, who enjoyed a couple of Top 40 albums in the late Seventies. Some believed he'd been a frontman for the Mafia; others believed he had got involved in drug running during his early days in order to get his own company, McGhee Entertainment, off the ground. Doc's introduction to the big time came in 1983, when he agreed to bank-roll a glam metal band from LA with no real songs to speak of but, as he put it, "more attitude than Hitler". None of the established management organisations were prepared to dirty their hands on Mötley Crüe, but they were ripping it up and drawing bigger and bigger crowds wherever they played.

When Mötley Crüe's first major-label album, 'Shout At The Devil', came out in 1983 and immediately sold two million copies in the US, Doc found himself in the enviable position of having the record companies ringing him wanting to know what he was going to do next. The first time he clapped his beady eyes on Jon and found himself tapping his calculator to the 'Runaway' demo, Doc knew what to tell them: Bon Jovi.

For the next three years, as 'The Doc' successfully guided first Mötley Crüe and then Bon Jovi to new million-dollar heights, stories regularly circulated about how he would go on the road with one of his bands, ostensibly in order to make sure everything was going smoothly, yet spend so much time partying that his partner, the much more low-key Doug Thaler, would have to follow Doc around clearing up after him. Eventually the strain of working with Doc proved too much for the phlegmatic Thaler, and in 1989 he dissolved his partnership with McGhee, taking Mötley Crüe with him, while Doc remained to oversee Bon Jovi's burgeoning business affairs.

The question on everybody's lips, of course, was did Jon and the band know anything about Doc's drug

Top: Doc McGhee in Russia; below: Richie and Jon flank Mötley Crüe's Nikki Six.

54

connections? Certainly there has never been any evidence to suggest that any member of Bon Jovi was ever involved in any illegal operations that may or may not have originated from Doc's office in the early Eighties. The original offence had, after all, occurred in 1982, before Bon Jovi had been signed to McGhee Entertainment. Whether Jon knew about Doc's shady past, though, and merely turned a blind eye to it is harder to answer.

Publicly, Jon's attitude towards drugs has always been of the Just Say No variety. In 1987, he had even taken part in the Rock Against Drugs campaign – a famous series of commercials screened nightly by MTV in America – which featured pop and movie celebrities warning their audience about the dangers of substance abuse. "I think this is a very important thing to do," Jon explained at the time. "I see a lot of kids in my travels. Most of them don't know what they're doing with their lives. I can understand where they're from. I've been there myself. I don't want to sound like I'm preaching or anything. I just want to share my experiences."

Jon was certainly no angel. Like most kids of his generation, he had done his share of drugs. But he wasn't a devotee. Weed gave him the willies. "When I was very young, I used to do a lot of drugs. It started out with just drinking beer at High School, and you puff on a joint. But then one night I must have smoked some bad pot or something... I kept hallucinating. It was awful. In the end I was rushed to hospital by the parents of a friend..." Cocaine had been OK "for about 10 minutes" in the only half-remembered daze of the mammoth 'Slippery...' tour... "back when I was too stupid or too tired to know the difference."

Whatever the truth behind the allegations about his manager, these were largely unsubstantiated rumours at the time. If Jon had heard them whispered more than once he may well have placed them in his mind alongside the many untold backgrounds and grey

origins of the people he had met since becoming a singer. What influential figure in the music business wasn't there a strange tale or two to tell about?

Once McGhee had been arrested, what was Jon to do? On the one hand, he could stand by his manager and risk being tarred with the same brush; accused of tacitly supporting Doc's drug smuggling past. On the other hand, he could distance himself and the band from Doc, perhaps even sever the contractual connections, but what then of his much-vaunted commitment to seeing Bon Jovi as a family? The test of a family's strength is how it stands by each other in times of great difficulty. And that's what Jon decided to do. Issuing his own statement to the press, Jon said he in no way condoned what his manager had done in the past, but made it clear that he himself saw no reason to further vilify him.

Convicted for his part in an international drug smuggling offence, the biggest surprise was the leniency of the judge's sentence. Doc got off with an absurdly lightweight $15,000 fine, a five-year suspended prison term and a lengthy period of 'community service', which his high-priced lawyers plea-bargained down to the setting up of a 'foundation' to fight drug abuse, to be called the 'Make A Difference Foundation'. Now the eyebrows were raised. But this time more from mirth than censure. It was the second time the McGhee organisation had been involved in apparently turning the American judicial system on its pointy head. In 1984, Mötley Crüe vocalist, Vince Neil, had been convicted after the car he was driving collided with on-coming traffic on the Los Angeles freeway, injuring three people, including his passenger, Hanoi Rocks drummer, Razzle, who died on his way to the hospital. Vince admitted he had been drunk at the wheel and was duly convicted of 'vehicular manslaughter'. Anybody else could have expected a sentence of up to 20 years in prison, but after more McGhee-

The Bon Jovi boys in Red Square.

style plea-bargaining, Neil eventually served just 30 days in an open prison in California, the bulk of his sentence deferred to 'community service', which basically amounted to a brace of TV commercials warning youngsters about the perils of drink-driving.

Having Vince Neil telling you not to get in a car and drive if you have been drinking alcohol may be as good a way as any of warning kids not to do something dangerous and stupid, but there was genuine outrage in some quarters at the apparent leniency of the sentencing. There was a certain sense of déjà-vu then, when – caught red-handed smuggling millions of dollars worth of illegal drugs into the US – Doc McGhee had got off with putting on a couple of multi-band concerts to raise money; hardly a stretch for the seasoned wheeler-dealer. The Doc, wily as ever, managed to fulfil his sentence at the same time as raising the profiles of his own artists in Russia, a country then beginning to regain exposure to the commercial whims of the Western world, and quickly identified by the buck-eyed business-man as a potential gold mine for rock music in the years to come.

Hence, the Moscow Music Peace Festival, held over two days at the Olympic Lenin Stadium, on August 12 and 13, 1989. With all 'profits' earmarked for Doc's newly instated Makes A Difference Foundation, he even tried to draw a comparison with the historic Woodstock festival held almost 20 years ago to the day, but even the shining-eyed MTV presenters had a job swallowing that one without choking.

Exactly how much was actually handed over to the Make A Difference trustees has never been revealed, though Jon is adamant that any money Bon Jovi might have made out of the trip all went to the Foundation. "We made nothing from the trip – in fact, we lost out, if anything," he said.

Bon Jovi, the jewel in Doc's gutter-crown, would headline, of course, and they would be joined by other good-intentioned members of the McGhee Entertainment clan like Mötley Crüe, Skid Row, and The Scorpions. The only acts on the bill not at least partially managed by The Doc were former Black Sabbath singer Ozzy Osbourne (a huge star behind the Iron Curtain and an important addition to a bill otherwise largely unfamiliar to most young Muscovites) and Cinderella (one of Jon's discoveries). Even the token Russian band, Gorky Park, had just signed an agreement with McGhee Entertainment.

To coincide with their first appearance in Russia, Doc had engineered a deal for the 'New Jersey' album with the official state label, Melodiya, for which he received the princely sum of $9,600. Peanuts by Western standards, it was, in fact, the first time Melodiya had released any legal – i.e. paid for – recordings by a Western artist. (In the past they'd simply released what in the West would be regarded as pirate recordings by Led Zeppelin, the Stones and Creedence Clearwater Revival, amongst others.) A compilation album was also put together for general world-wide release called 'Stairway To Heaven/Highway To Hell', featuring the artists involved in the Moscow shows and others doing cover versions of favourite songs by bands that had

suffered terrible losses because of the twin demons of drink and drugs. Bon Jovi's contribution was 'The Boys Are Back In Town' by Thin Lizzy, whose singer-song-writer, Phil Lynott, died of drug-related causes in 1985, and which was a staple of the band's live set since their earliest days. "Phil Lynott was a genius," Jon has told me on more than one occasion. "I just wish that those people who were around him when he was in really bad shape because of the heroin or whatever, I just wish one of them could have said or done something. Just told him it wasn't cool any more, you know?"

I was there filming a documentary on the shows for Sky TV and spent a fair bit of time following Jon and the band around, getting their reactions to the city and the event. "You know, at this stage of the game, it's like you ask yourself what can we do that Zeppelin or the Stones or The Beatles didn't do already, and being here is it," Jon replied when I asked what he thought an event like this could actually achieve, in real terms. "People are always ready to question the motives behind why a bunch of rock stars would want to get together and do something like this. And sure, inevitably you get a clash of egos, occasionally. It's not exactly the easiest thing in the world to organise.

"But at the end of the day, I look at it like this. I wouldn't have known about Nelson Mandela's situation like I do now had I not been drawn to it because of the artists who took part in the Amnesty International bills. Or I don't think that I'd have ever known about Ethiopia the way I do now, if it wasn't for Bob Geldof and Live Aid.

"So, there's a wonderful icing on the cake. You get to see all these big performers that I enjoy too, but there's ultimately a cause behind it. And that's what raises your awareness."

The last time I saw Jon on that trip he was standing in Red Square looking lost. "Have you discovered any of the night life here yet?" he asked. I shook my head. "What's Richie up to?" I asked, thinking he would be the one to ask where the action was. Jon stared at me like he didn't know who I was talking about. I changed the subject.

There was certainly little sign of peace anywhere else at the festival. McGhee himself seemed to see the event less as a penance he was being forced to pay and more a sort of affirmation of his own pre-eminence. Not all his artists were so convinced, however. There was a nasty altercation between Mötley drummer, Tommy Lee, and Doc McGhee during Bon Jovi's set on the first day because of a row over whether Mötley should go on before or after Ozzy Osbourne. Doc said before Ozzy; Mötley said after. They went on before.

The nonsense that went on behind the scenes at the Moscow Music Peace Festival put the first serious nail into the coffin of the Doc's relationship with his most successful client, Jon. If there had been signs of tension between the two before the concerts, privately Jon let it be known afterwards that as far as he was concerned, Bon Jovi had been used by their manager.

But it was to be Skid Row who cast the biggest shadow over Bon Jovi's career, in those days, and in the process created a controversy that would rage for years.

8

" I knocked him onto his little butt. But then I picked him up and hugged him. He was just too arrogant for his own good. Something had to be done about it. " (on Sebastian Bach)

ON THE SKIDS

Sebastian Bach:
" For the record, I don't shoot heroin... "

By Spring of 1988 they had signed a long-term contract with Atlantic Records. Shortly after they commenced writing and recording their first album with veteran hairspray producer (White Lion, Mötley Crüe) Michael Wagener. Recorded in Lake Geneva, Wisconsin (" We wanted to be able to zone in on what we were doing," drummer Rob Affuso recalled), the 'Skid Row' album was released on January 23, 1989. To coincide with its appearance, Bon Jovi offered them the much-coveted support slot on their prestigious 'New Jersey' world tour – an opportunity they still admit gave them the break that was to help make them superstars. The first album sold in its millions – not least because of all the good singles lifted from it – both the anthemic 'Youth Gone Wild' and the hilariously po-faced ballad, 'I Remember You', had secured the band hit status. But it was the first track from the album, '18 And Life', that clinched their place in history as songwriters worth something more than the cars- and-crotch-shots mentality of most of their contemporaries. The first ever Skid Row single was, simply, a classic rock song in every sense. Neither ballad nor out-and-out ball-buster, it was a heady combination of the two, mixed in with something not often found in mid-Eighties rock music – a song with a good story.

Some say Jon had more than a hand in helping to write the songs on that first album, and certainly '18 And Life' is the sort of manicured 'wedding cake' (layers and layers that build and build) production that JBJ patented with 'Livin' On A Prayer' and 'Wanted: Dead Or Alive'.

Both lyrically and musically, '18 And Life' is completely out of synch with the rest of the hard-hitting 'Skid Row' album. It is delicate, mature and blessed with so many of the trademarks that Jon and Richie had virtually made their own. Is it too excessive to suggest that it could easily have slotted onto the 'New Jersey' album? I think not.

"With the Skids, that was something I'd been working on for two years," Jon later confessed to the author. "For about a year-and-a-half of that we were writing songs with them, re-writing songs, paying for studio time, paying their rent and every single thing that came with them..."

At the time who knew the truth... and who cared. A damn good band had broken into the mainstream. And they had a frontman with personality-plus. Said Sebastian musing on the aftershock of '18 And Life' and what it meant to a lot of the people who bought it: "I don't want some kid to read this and go out and get rotted just because I did. It's just that where I grew up drugs were in your face from a very early age. I probably smoked my first joint when I was 12. I don't want to be a hypocrite about this. I know some bands who swear they don't do nothin' to the press, then just party their fuckin' nuts off every chance they get on whatever's going, you know?

"For the record, I don't shoot heroin... After a show, I smoke a couple of joints, have a couple of beers, a couple of pulls of Jack Daniel's. No big deal, you know? I'm cool."

And it had all started out with Jon trying to do an old mate a big favour...

Jon took time out during the promotional stint for 'Slippery When Wet' to extol the virtues of his friend's band: "They are one of the most exciting young bands that I've seen recently and I am doing what I can to help them along. I genuinely believe they can go a long way in this business."

While Skid Row might arguably have made it big without the massive help they received from the Bon Jovi camp, the fact is they didn't make it on their own. And up until their second album, 'Slave To The Grind' (1991), Jon's influence cast a very long shadow indeed over everything the Skids achieved.

Formed in 1987, primarily by Jon's old pal, guitarist Dave 'The Snake' Sabo, and bassist Rachel Bolan, their big influence when they were starting out was Kiss (to this day Skid Row will warm up with a version of 'Room Service' from Kiss' 1975 'Dressed To Kill' album). The line-up only really stabilised though with the arrival of Canadian-born, blond-haired, self-styled "Heavy Metal Viking from hell!", Sebastian Bach, who had previously "tried out" as vocalist in "too many fucking bands to mention", including an early unrecorded incarnation of Madam X, helping to pay the rent with occasional beer commercials on Canadian TV. The bulk of the material that eventually made its way onto the first eponymously titled Skid Row album was already written by the time Sebastian arrived on the scene, but that didn't prevent him from going out and getting the title to one of them – 'Youth Gone Wild' – tattooed in elaborately stencilled letters up the length of his right forearm the day after he joined the band.

It wasn't long, however, before Sebastian was writing his own "one hundred per cent autobiographical" lyrics. "I don't need to make nothin' up," he boasted the first time I interviewed him. "It's not a fake thing. It's not some 35-year-old guy singing, I'm a youth gone wild! I was 19 when I recorded this song, you know? I fuckin' mean that shit..." 'Making A Mess' was his first group composition. "I used to fuckin' smoke cocaine and drink Scotch before I went to school when I was 15. Needless to say, school didn't last too long..."

Richie (left) with Skid Row's Dave 'Snake' Sebo and former Riot and Pat Travers drummer Sandy Gennaro.

Jon and Skid Row's Sebastian Bach before the falling out.

But suddenly, things turned sour in this seemingly idyllic relationship. Rumours began to spread that Skid Row had knowingly signed over the publishing rights to all their songs to Jon and Richie. This was in return for all the favours bestowed on them, from helping write the songs that put them in the charts to launching their career as a major concert attraction. In the case of an act as successful as Skid Row, such a deal would mean millions of dollars being diverted away from the band. However, there was no suggestion that the band had been hoodwinked in any way into the situation. The problems started when Sebastian began to complain about the deal to members of the British rock press.

It was even suggested that as a result of Sebastian's growing dissatisfaction, he had gone AWOL from the band for a time, telling everybody that he had quit Skid Row, and privately offering his services to Guns N' Roses, themselves going through one of their periodic on-off-on-again bust ups with temperamental singer, Axl Rose.

Then, in November 1990, while Sebastian was back at home in New Jersey, he was shaken to read in an interview Jon had done to promote his forthcoming solo album, 'Blaze Of Glory: Music From The Soundtrack Of Young Guns II', that he said that he and Sebastian had come to blows when Skid Row were on tour with Bon Jovi in America. "Things got to such a point that, in the end, I knocked him onto his little butt. But then I picked him up and hugged him," Jon told *RAW*. "He was just being too arrogant for his own good. Something had to be done about it."

Sebastian was straight onto the phone to the magazine, bitterly complaining that Jon had never laid a hand on him. "He claimed that after one show where Sebastian had slagged Jon off on stage, that Jon had confronted Sebastian with one of his younger brothers and two burly security guards in tow," Malcolm Dome, the writer he spoke to, told me. "Baz claimed that Jon threatened him, but that when he offered to fight Jon one-on-one there and then, Jon chickened out."

"Jon had his brother and several bodyguards with him," Sebastian insisted when I spoke to him. "He got them to pin me against a wall, and then threatened me. He stood there wagging his finger and lecturing. Well, I was quite prepared to take him on, but not with the others with him. So, I told him that if he wanted to step into a room by himself, then I would have punched him out. No problem. Who do you think would have won? A lightweight Bruce Springsteen fan or a heavyweight Metallica maniac like me." The rant went on. In the midst of these impromptu tirades, however, Sebastian openly attacked Jon for "stealing from Skid Row". The singer actually came out and accused Jon of "ripping off money that rightfully belonged to Skid Row".

"He has $70 million in his bank account, but he seems to be desperate to get an extra $2 million from us. Why, I don't know. But he has us under a publishing contract whereby we make nothing at all. And I promise you that unless things change we will not carry on. I'd rather split this band up than carry on making money for Jon Bon Jovi."

Richie and Pete.

The words 'shit' and 'fan' had never been quite so closely aligned in connection with the name Bon Jovi. What made it worse was the claim that Richie had been embarrassed by the situation and had actually handed back the share of the money he'd made to Skid Row. "What happened was that I was part of a company with Jon, but disagreed with what was going on. So, I gave back some money and got out," was his muted explanation.

But the question remained: Just what had gone on? Had Jon done something unethical by expecting to be repaid for the job he did in making the band into huge international stars?

When Bon Jovi took Cinderella under their wing, it was apparently done with no thought for financial reward. But had he been employed as an A&R man at PolyGram to do the amazing job he did on making Cinderella big, then he would have earned a great deal of money for his efforts. As it is, he earned nothing from the success of a band that were lucky if they could get two gigs on consecutive nights in their native Philadelphia before Jon Bon Jovi decided that they had what it takes and personally went out of his way to tell everybody so.

So when it came to Skid Row, Jon understandably decided to put the whole relationship on a more professional footing. It was a delicate situation, dealing with friends is difficult enough when it comes to creative pursuits; often too many things are taken for granted. Also, that way, Jon was ensured that Dave never felt he was accepting a hand-out from an old friend. Jon wasn't doing anybody any favours. He genuinely thought Skid Row had what it takes and he was prepared to put his money where his mouth was and back them for two years.

Jon was considerably more involved in the first Skid Row album than he has ever admitted. Malcolm Dome pointed out that by securing the publishing royalties on that first Skid Row album, "Jon would have been making back the money he himself could have earned by keeping it for a Bon Jovi album."

Moreover, Dome is prepared to speculate that any decision along these lines was taken before Sebastian was recruited, so that he would never have been part of the agreement process.

When I talked to Sebastian about it in 1989, he was still extremely heated up about things, though. "People say, 'Oh you guys wouldn't have made it without Bon Jovi'. I go, 'Who knows?' I don't know. I don't think anybody, though, if they were offered the fuckin' biggest tour in the world with the biggest management in the world, with a big record contract, I can't see 'em going, 'No, no, I don't think so, I think I'm gonna wait around a couple more years and do it all my way', you know? Fuck that shit, man! Most guys my age would give their left nut to do what we've been doing this year.

"This is the way it is... 'Snake' grew up with Jon. Their backyards faced each other in New Jersey when they were kids. They were always big buddies. You know, they got laid for the first time together at the same party. And they got drunk together for the first time. They were like fuckin' best friends, right?

Then, when they both started getting involved in bands, they kind of made this pact. You know like, 'If you make it first, man, I'll fuckin' come back and help you', and vice versa, you know?

"Which was pretty fuckin' cool for the rest of us in the band! Fuck yeah, you did the right thing that day, Snake old buddy!" he laughed.

And the song publishing a gle...?

He spat on the carpet. "Jeez it's on the album, isn't it? If you look at the fine print, I mean, yeah, that's what happened, man... Things like that happen to everybody in this business. I had to pay a former manager, when I joined Skid Row, like $20,000. Just to be fuckin' in this band. And I mean, I didn't have that kind of money. I'd never sold any records. But Jon gave me that money to pay this guy off, or I couldn't have been in this band."

On the fisticuffs, Sebastian: "What really happened was, it was the end of the tour and the road crew decided it was gag night, right? Maybe we took our little gag too far, I don't know. I mean, we did the same thing at the beginning of the tour and there was no comeback from his end or anything. I was grabbed just as I was about to go on stage. Somebody poured a gallon of freezing cold ice-milk over me! But the intro tape was rolling and I just had to go on there covered in all this shit...

"So I go out there – big gag – and when I get to the mike I go into this rant against Jon. Like, come on up here, pussy, and get a piece of me, motherfucker! And all this shit. But see, he's my friend and it's like, that's our sense of humour, you know? But I guess in front of 20,000 people that maybe don't get the joke, it looked kinda heavy. I mean, I watched the tape back and it came over really fuckin' harsh an' all. It was like a riot was gonna start.

"But, you know, this is my first tour. I don't know all the rules to these games yet. Then it turned out that Jon didn't know anything about what his road crew had done to me. And he got pissed off and when we came offstage we had a fight... I never wanna say this, though. I'll never back down from a fight. Anybody comes near me, they're gonna get a fuckin' kick in the head. And that's the way I'm gonna leave it... That's all there is to say.

"But I still love Jon and thank him for the best year of my life."

To accuse Jon of "stealing" from him, as Sebastian did, was misleading, to say the least. Besides, surely if Dave Sabo felt the same way he would have done or said something about it by now. Instead, he and Jon have remained close friends.

Eventually the controversial publishing contract was amended to ensure that the Skids got their due from future recordings. True, relations between Jon and Sebastian have remained entirely strained; to this day there's still bad blood between the parties concerned. But the pair are such differing personalities that it's doubtful they could ever be close friends anyway. But there were other problems looming for Bon Jovi – and this time they came from within the band, not from an outside source.

❝ I want us to be together. It's really been my love and I feel a loyalty to those guys...❞

NO SMOKE...

❝ Things are not happy in the Bon Jovi camp, they're not happy at all. ❞

❝ We had to fight even on the 'New Jersey' album to prove that we were gonna be around. ❞

By the start of 1990, despite the fame and despite the fortune, Bon Jovi as a working line-up had reached 'burn out'. Desperately in need of a rest after the rigours of practically five years without a decent break, Jon the workaholic was the only one who actually wanted to keep going, to keep pushing back the envelope.

The rest of the band did not and suddenly the unhappy whiff of mutiny was in the air. "Truthfully, I still don't know what was going on. I think I've, like, blanked it out," Richie smilingly tried to side-step the issue when we last met. "Everyone was so burnt out. I could just about make it to the stage. Everybody was concerned. It was strange. I went from like the highest point to the lowest point of our careers together."

Or, as Tico told the author: "When we broke up for that small while, I totally stopped playing. I'd been doing it for 20-something years, but I turned off the radio and put the sticks down. I worked on cars and boats – anything creative besides music. I sorta lived like a hermit, in that sense. But sometimes the best thing you can do is stop, because then you can start to appreciate things again."

Jon was asked to participate in putting together a soundtrack for the film, *Young Guns II*. Normally, he might not have given it a second thought, but with the band exhausted, Jon turned his full attention to making something of this movie offer. The first *Young Guns* film had been a huge hit and something of a brat-pack special, starring Emilio Estevez and Keifer Sutherland. The follow-up, once again starring many of the hottest young talents in Hollywood, promised to be one of the biggest movies of the year.

Truly out on his own for the first time in his career, it was clear that Jon had taken the project very seriously indeed. He was, despite all his protestations to the contrary, determined that his first solo outing should not be any less spectacular a success than any other 'Bon Jovi' record.

The album itself was written solely by Jon, who also produced it himself in association with the veteran West Coast session guitarist Danny Kortchmar. Jon's selection further underpinned his credibility and pulling power. It was also a warning shot to the rest of the band as to how he was being perceived by the big wheels.

The big hit from 'Blaze Of Glory' was the title track, which had all the hallmarks of classic Bon Jovi – in itself worrying for the other four. Suddenly, here was Jon making a formidable hit single without them!

Elsewhere on the album, the fierce 'Billy Get Your Guns', the more contemplative 'Miracle', the quick-draw 'Justice In The Barrel', the slowly cynical 'Dyin' Ain't Much Of A Livin'' and the almost visually arresting drama of 'Santa Fe' proved to be master strokes. Jon on his own had made a great Bon Jovi album, which suggested the band as it stood was redundant.

'Blaze Of Glory' sold more than two million copies in the US alone, though with the exception of 'Blaze...', hardly any of it made it to the final screen-edit of the movie. When the film was released, I interviewed Jon in New York. We talked on the roof top of McGhee Entertainment, a suite of offices on the second floor of a building overlooking Central Park. I began by asking about what was then his new single, 'Blaze Of Glory'.

This is your first solo record, right?

"No! I've gotta keep saying that. I don't want anyone thinking this is a solo thing. I have to re-state it time and time again. This is a soundtrack. It's for a movie. And that's all it's supposed to be. I mean, I had to write it to fit a certain parameter. So, I don't want anyone thinking this is a solo anything. It's not. The parameters I had to write under were so limiting, you know. I could only write songs for particular scenes that some other guy came up with.

"I have to keep re-stating that 'cos I don't want anyone reviewing the album as if this is a solo album and I can only write about this."

How did it come about?

"Well, how it started was they wanted to use 'Wanted: Dead Or Alive' in the movie. I was told that they wrote the first *Young Guns* with 'Wanted...' in mind, that it was a big influence on the movie, and I was really flattered. I like the first *Young Guns* movie a lot, and I always said that if I'd ever acted in a movie it would have been in *Young Guns*."

Were you ever approached to be in the first movie?

"No, no, not at all. But anyway, it turns out they decide they wanna feature 'Wanted...' on the soundtrack to the follow-up. Lyrically, though, it wouldn't have worked. You know, 'On a steel horse I ride...'. It just doesn't fit the movie. So I said, if you want I'll write you something in that vein to fit this part of the movie. I knew where it was going, they told me what it was about, and I went there with a song in hand, which was 'Blaze Of Glory'. I wrote it just by what they told me over the phone.

"So, I took it to 'em. They liked it. And then I came home and wrote three more. So now we've got four songs, all based on what they'd told me about the movie. So, they said, 'Great, let's do an album'."

But isn't it true that you were looking for some form of solo expression outside of the band anyway?

"I honest to God had no intention whatsoever of doing a solo venture, because to me Bon Jovi records are my solo albums. There's not any songs really that I adamantly didn't want on any of the Bon Jovi records. If I didn't want something, it wasn't there. I mean, my interpretation of what was going to happen to us as we had these discussions in January, was that we were gonna go home and Richie was going to do his solo record. It was gonna be Richie Sambora & Friends. It was gonna be all his friends playing cover songs, playing some of his songs, playing some things that me and him do together.

"Meantime, Dave was gonna do a New Age record and I was gonna mix the Bon Jovi live album. And that was what the year was gonna be. That was the plan anyway. But come February, when the tour was ending, the one thing in my mind was, if something comes up that you don't do every day of your life, do it this time. For the first time, when you say you're going to do something, go out and fucking do it! Like, if you finally want to go somewhere where there isn't an arena, then go there, you know? Like, I always say I wanna go to Utah and ride motorcycles and I never fucking do...

"So when Emilio Estevez was so adamant about me coming out there I said, 'Fuck it, I'm gonna get on an aeroplane without the band, without my road manager, without my wife, all by myself and go and do this'. That was a big step for me, to go and do something by myself."

He stared out at the yellow taxi cabs circling for fares.

"It's a big deal for me to come to New York City, an hour-and-a-half from my house, without picking' up my dad on the way and saying. 'Hey, you wanna take a ride?' Which is what I did today... I'm not used to doing anything by myself. I just don't do it."

Are you pleased with the results of the 'Blaze Of Glory...' album?

"I'm very excited by the album. By playing with those guys. Even if I didn't play with those guys, I was real excited to just get up, 'cos I wanted to get up, write 10 songs for an album, go produce it and have people be happy with it.

"When I did it, I was excited. When the single came out over here, I was waiting with baited breath to see what would happen. Just like I always am before I release a record. But now that it's out, it's beyond me. So now there's a sigh of relief and what happens, happens."

How did the big names end up on the album?

"Why them? It was the idea that... Well, I've always loved Jeff Beck's playing and I loved his sound. So the idea was, who would you get to play on 'Blaze Of Glory'? It wasn't a matter of four songs or 10 songs, it was one song. My first choice of guitar player was Jeff Beck. I mean if you're shooting for something you may as well aim for the sky, you know."

You had met before, hadn't you?

"Yeah. He's been to some shows. He'd been to Wembley, he'd been to Hammersmith, he'd been to see us before, yeah. I thought he was a nice enough guy, so what the hell, give him a call and see what he says. He said yes so quickly and hung up the phone that I wouldn't have sworn he was coming. He was like, 'I'd love to do it, man. Have your manager call my manager. It sounds like a great idea. And, er, I gotta go'. I was like, yeah, sure, man. We've all heard the rumours about what he's like, you know.

"Well, the fucker not only flew out to LA to do it, but he was in the studio in the morning before I was and wouldn't leave until I physically said, 'I'm not gonna do this anymore, go home!' I mean, he worked his ass off! He dispelled all the rumours about him, he was a consummate professional."

What's he like as a person outside of the studio?

"Jeff's a little boy. He loves to play. He wants to go to the movies. We went to see *Total Recall* together. And he loves to drive around in his car. He wants to go out to dinner and goof off. I mean, he loves to go play around, but when it came time to work, he was right there on the money every time."

Were you nervous working with him?

"No, you see, because... though I like Jeff Beck, I didn't buy his records when I was a kid. He was a great sounding guitar player, but for me it was always

Rod Stewart. I was a singer. I played guitar to write songs. I never grew up wanting to be Jeff. I wanted to grow up and be Rod Stewart."

What about Elton John?

"Ah... again, there's a guy that's a songwriter, consummate songwriter and performer, and Elton is a great guy as well. Fortunately, I got a feeling meeting Elton – I think the first time was when he came to see us – I got a feeling meeting Elton that he was one of the guys. He was a real sweetheart who just loves playing piano.

"Then I played with him at Madison Square Garden and I felt that I had a friend in Elton. When he was in Los Angeles at that time, I thought that he would be perfect. It wasn't name-value so much as the fact that he was perfect for the part. Roy Bitten [E-Street Band keyboard player] was booked, but Bruce Springsteen would not let him do it."

Why, because it was you?

"I don't think so. I think he's co–producing his album."

It wasn't a bit of New Jersey-boy rivalry?

"If Bruce Springsteen is afraid of me, then I'm flattered. But I doubt that this is the case. I think that it's just purely that Roy's co–producing the Springsteen album and he couldn't do it. But with Elton being there, he said he'd love to do it.

"So, I had him come over and one song in particular that I wrote on piano really lent itself to Elton – 'Dyin' Ain't Much Of A Livin'. To me it sounds like an Elton John song, he sings on it. To me it was like he's the only guy who can play this song. Then in the control room he started to sing the harmony. All along I was dying to get him to sing the harmony and he started doing it, so there was my way in. I went, 'Hey, why don't you sing it?' So we did it live and the vocal was right there."

You were a big Elton John fan when you were growing up?

"Like, the biggest! When he was on the cover of *Time* magazine in '74 or '75, I remember in grammar school as a class project I made a red, white and blue guitar and wrote 'Elton' on it. I had the 'Caribou' album and 'Goodbye Yellow Brick Road'. That whole era, he was the biggest to me. I listened to him religiously.

"So to have him play on it was real exciting. Then in an old art deco fifties–ish diner, right next to the studio – this was prior to Jeff flying in – we said, 'Who else can we get?' Just joking around. Like, what legends are there left in the business? And we thought, Keith Richards. Let's get Keith!

"The one thing about Keith was everyone in the room played guitar, everyone, me, Aldo Nova and everyone fought to play on the record. finally, I said to Danny Kortchmar, 'Who's record is this, man? It's mine. I'm playing the parts'. It's like everyone wanted to play on this record. I said, 'Let's get Little Richard to play this song' and everyone dropped their cheeseburgers. Like, 'You know Little Richard?' I said, 'Yeah I do, he played with us on the last tour'.

"So I called him up and he came down and it was fucking great 'cos it was the one thing I could do... Jeff Beck knows the Stones, The Beatles, he's played

Top: Jon with Masin Star buddy Emelio Estevez at the première for the film Blown Away; below: with Elton John.

Jon auditions for a part in Mr Ed with the original star.

Is there going to be another Bon Jovi album?

"I hope so. But I don't know so. And I can publicly say it to you, because the truth is the British press started this whole fucking fiasco. We were in Mexico, at the end of the tour, with nothing but wonderful things happening. We were finishing the tour, doing stadiums, which is just how we wanted to end, and we were feeling real good. Then *Kerrang!* says Tico is leaving the band. Suddenly we got drummer tapes and pictures and everything comin' in. It was like, 'Hey Tico, are you quitting the band?' He was like, 'first I've heard of it, man'.

"That was amazing. That's when it started, but we pushed it away. I threw the magazine out the window. I was upset 'cos I knew it wasn't true. I think the quotes were like the drummer's quitting and the band is breaking up. I thought, 'What the fuck's this?'

"So then the English papers, I think it was *The Sun* or one of those gossip rags, got hold of it. The headline ran 'All Ovi For Bon Jovi'. It said that Richie Sambora was out and there were money problems, that he wasn't happy with his cut and he was leaving for Cher and all this shit. I'm reading it out of the fax, thinking: what is all this shit?

"Then the phone calls start coming in, people calling me saying they want the gig. I tell you, four months later I'm not entertained by it any more. It's got to this point because the five of us haven't been in the same room together since before the last show and it's added fuel to the fire. So now all of us are believing there are problems. I can't tell you what the problems are about, but we think we've got problems."

But you and Richie have grown apart?

"In the state of things at this time, yeah. Right now, in July 1990, yeah. Things are not happy in the Bon Jovi camp, that's for sure, they're not happy at all. I don't want the band to break up, 'cos the five of us... You can only play your first time at Donington once. Your first – what was it – the Dominion, in London. Those gigs were what made us. We were spitting in the eye of the fire and we didn't give a fuck about anyone. It was us and we were gonna make it.

"Regardless ~~of~~ money and stadiums, or who I played with, if that was the band tomorrow and Elton was my new keyboard player, it would never be the same. All of that would be lost and I don't want that to happen. I definitely do not want that to happen. I want to keep it together, 'cos these are the guys who seven years ago were here when we sat on this ledge for the first time, when we didn't have enough money for a pretzel across the street and no-one knew whether Bon Jovi was jeans or what the fuck it was.

"We had to fight for everything we got and we had to fight even on the 'New Jersey' album to prove that we were gonna be around. It's a rewarding feeling to know that the band as a unit did this. I could play with better musicians, or different musicians and they could play with a better songwriter and singer, but it wouldn't be the same, ever."

Does everyone have to get their solo albums out of their system?

with everybody. But he asked me to introduce him to Little Richard, so I did. I asked him to introduce me to Rod Stewart and he did that.

"So I called Richard and he came down and Jeff was so excited and nervous. When Richard walked into the control room – and I know this 'cos I've done it myself, you feel foolish afterwards – but Jeff couldn't help himself and when Richard walked into the control room his fingers started playing 'Lucille'.

"Richard put his hand out to me and Jeff jumps out of his seat and gives him his hand and says, 'It's so nice to meet you. You're the reason I got into this business', and asks him for his autograph. You have to slap yourself once in a while and say, my life is so lucky that I get to be in the company of people like this. To watch these things happen is just a thrill."

What happened to the Keith Richards idea?

"Well, with five guitar players already, we decided to just steal his licks instead."

"I don't know, you'd have to ask them. Richie was always, 'Oh, I'm gonna do it' to the point where things weren't happening for him and he joined this thing.

"Everyone gives Rich a lot of attention – and well – deserved it is, he's a fine musician and a fine singer – but I don't think it's fair to harp on him all the time, because it was us and the band. For the first two albums, he never wrote any of the singles.

Dave Bryan co-wrote the singles. It was Dave and I who did it. Richie came in on the third album when he had begun to understand the way I like to write. It wasn't until the third album, so it's not fair for everyone to pick on him because... the press I mean, it's not fair."

You and Richie are the stars of the show, though.

"It's so stereotypical of what's supposed to be, though... John Lennon and Paul McCartney, it's the same thing."

If a lead guitarist leaves a band it's bigger news than a drummer leaving...

"Yeah, right. I don't know how much I like that or dislike that, but it's true. I missed him very much when Little Steven left Bruce, it just wasn't the same any more. I don't want this band to break up. But there aren't any plans to make a record at the moment."

Where does that leave your career?

"Promoting the *Young Guns* record first and foremost. Promoting the *Young Guns* record as a soundtrack for a movie, and then I'm going to go and produce other things and get them out.

Sooner or later, you'll want to get back on the road, though?

"Yes, I love touring. I absolutely love it. I went to see Alec and he said to me, 'The Alec that was out there in South America and Mexico isn't the guy that you know now...'. I didn't think he was being any weirder than usual but he says, 'I was so burned, I couldn't take it any more, but you wanted to keep going, so we had to keep going'. I didn't know what to say. I felt great this tour, so I kept pushing and pushing. I didn't give a shit. I'd have stayed out there forever."

Do you have difficulty switching off, perhaps?

"No, I love touring, but I can turn it off. When I'm done touring, I'm done. I don't have any desire to go down the Stone Pony [club in New Jersey] on a Sunday night and play a song. I don't have any desire to do that at all.

"I'm really excited by the avenue that's opened up though, doing this soundtrack. And I'm blown away that Darryl Hall and John Oates have recently asked me to work with them (as a songwriter and producer). I was even happier afterwards when they would tell people, 'He's a real producer'. I guess coming from them, that's a compliment."

He talked a little about his plans for his own label; acknowledged that he probably wouldn't be lending a hand to the next Skid Row album. Then we turned back to the then just-released *Young Guns II*.

How did you end up in it?

"Oh, I'm in it for 30 seconds, don't mistake this for an acting career! I was freezing my ass off in Santa Fe, New Mexico in February, dressed the way you would dress your three-year-old kid, you know, snow-suit, gloves, feet warmers, just freezing my ass. I was thinking, 'Why am I out here with these idiots?' you know. I was miserable, while the stars of the movie are running around in T-shirts and jeans, riding horses, moving around, running, shooting and I'm going, 'Fuck this. I'm a spoiled brat. I wanna go home!'

"They said, 'Be in the movie', and I said, 'Great, give me something to do. I hate this!' And they did. So, for 30 seconds I escape from this jail with the writer of the movie, who was the fan who started all of this off. I escape from this jail with him. We grab the deputy in the jail. The sheriff sees me and loads up his gun and I take one hit to the chest and there's blood everywhere. It's in slow-motion and in close-up. And that's it. It took me longer to explain it than it did for it to happen."

Do you think there'll be teenage girls having heart attacks seeing Jon Bon Jovi splattered like that?

"Do you know what they're really gonna have heart attacks over? The seven bucks it costs them to get into the movie – 'cos I'm in it for 30 seconds, max! Nobody blink!"

But Hollywood is making a big deal of your presence in the movie...

"Tell me about it. I mean, I don't want 'em taking advantage of our fans, making believe like this is my first big film part or anything. Like the album. I'm pissed off because first they were gonna use at least four songs in the movie. Then it was three. Now I'm afraid that the last cut was only two. So here's gonna be my friends and fans and family going to see a movie that I'm in for 30 seconds and I have two songs in. But they're marketing it like it was my first major film role or something..."

What is it about the cowboy image – a familiar image from so many of your songs – that attracts you?

"I think it's that kind of lifestyle. The truth of the matter is, like the way we wrote 'Wanted: Dead Or Alive', I feel that you ride into town, you don't know where the fuck you are. You're with your 'gang'; stealing money; getting what you can off any girl that'll give it to you; drinking as much of the free alcohol as you can and being gone before the law catches you.

"Before someone wakes you from this wonderful dream and says, 'You're an asshole, you're going to jail'. Because it's not the real world I'm living in, it's a dream sequence, a big fucking wet dream."

Are you a nicer person now than five years ago?

"Maybe. I hope so. I think I'm a little more cynical and sceptical. I hope I am nicer, but you'd have to tell me that. Other people would have to tell me whether I am or not."

All I remember is a very energetic and excited kid.

"I still think I have a lot of energy and I am excited. That's probably another reason why the band is going their own ways. We are supposed to, like human beings do, take time off. I gotta settle down. The way I figure it is, if I was to sit with Freud or one of those guys, he'd tell me it was because I hate my wife or my mother

or something. Because all I like to do is go and work. I dig making records."

Have you consciously tried not to turn into an asshole?

"No. People will say about you what they want. I mean there's a DJ here in New York named Howard Stern who went on a rampage for about a year, saying what scumbags me and my organisation are. Because I couldn't go to his radio station the week 'Bad Medicine' came out. He literally went on a tirade for a year and it really upset me. I was a true friend of his.

"Then there's the good stories about how I helped a little girl across the street one day. Everyone's got their stories, you gotta deal with them. I just hope there's more good than bad."

Sebastian Bach doesn't seem to appreciate what you've done...

"At 22, I guess he doesn't. But I can punch the bastard in the face and be very happy I did it."

Does that make you less inclined to be charitable to support bands?

"No, definitely not, that would never happen. One thing that I heard someone say, I think it was Billy Squier, was 'If you're ever afraid of your support band, then you don't deserve to be headlining'. So I would give any support band anything to help them. It only makes the show better for the people who come to see us.

"I don't give a shit about the ego involved. All I expect is, like if this is my house then treat it nicely, don't spit in the house, you know? That's all I would ask of anyone; if you don't like us, then fine, go about your business, but don't ever slag it, because that's why you're here. Fortunately for us we don't need a support band – it's like whoever we want to put on the bill. When you're the one selling all the tickets, then who gives a shit? The you're doing it because they are your friends.

"The Skids are wonderful guys though. I just spent a week's vacation with 'Snake' and Rachel. I still love them very much – and Sebastian's probably a good kid, too. I don't spend enough time with him to find out.

"It's tough for him to grow out of my shadow. I mean, every fucking interview they were saying, 'Jon did this for you. Jon did that'. I'm sure he got sick of it, like, 'Fuck Jon!' I understand."

Who do you think from the bands today will still figure in 20 years?

"Prince will still be important. And Madonna. I think Madonna has been incredibly important to the Eighties, musically. She was a little disco queen who lost the babyfat and became an icon, an Eighties version of Marilyn Monroe."

What about Springsteen?

"I wanna hear Bruce's new stuff as much as anyone else, 'cos I wanna hear which way he goes. Nobody, except the people who've played on the record (who say it's real cool) have heard it yet. I don't know what Bruce means to everyone else. For someone from New Jersey that's not a fair question. He was the hometown boy, so to us he was Jesus when I was in high school. And nobody had heard of him when I was in high school. I really don't know about Bruce."

What about some of the classic rockers like Aerosmith?

"I don't know if they count or not. They been around for 17 years as it is. But they have influenced so many bands who came up when I did. Not us particularly, but Ratt and Mötley and all those kind of bands."

Guns N' Roses?

"Good question. They've still yet to be proven. I don't know whether Axl is a genius or a psycho. I've heard that this song 'Civil War' is amazing and I think that lyrically if he is going after that then he has real potential of being there."

Metallica?

"I don't know any of their music, except for that song 'One' which I saw on MTV. They were better than I previously thought they'd be. I've still never heard a Metallica record and I never saw them when I played with them. It's not that I'm not interested. I respect those guys a lot. But they have given Bon Jovi a lot of stick.

"I actually sent them a telegram when their bass player, Cliff Burton, got killed, because I knew that the bond that they have is similar to what we have and I really felt bad for them. Apparently, they never received it."

Mötley Crüe?

He eyed me; was I taking the piss now?

"I don't think that the Mötleys are at all influential. I don't think that they ever had enough to say lyrically, musically or personally. Again, because of the mud they've thrown over here, it made better press for them to slag us than to slag Doc McGhee, 'cos no-one knows who Doc is... All power to them, they just made their most popular record yet ['Dr. Feelgood'], but I don't think they'll stand the test of time."

What about Bon Jovi in 20 years' time?

"I want us to be together because it's afforded me all these things. It's really been my love and I feel a loyalty to those four guys that I only feel toward my immediate family. I hope that I can keep it together, but I'll only keep it together if it's fun. I can't do it for the money and I can't do it to keep the record company happy. I can't do it unless it is going to be a good time.

"Unless I still want to have a beer with those guys every night like we always have then..." He paused, squinting into the sun. "We always grew up hearing 'Boy, Van Halen were so dumb to split with David Lee Roth'. But none of us in the general public know what the real problem was. Same with Journey. Same with Aerosmith before they got back together.

"I'm giving you these examples so you can tell your readers that I'm as confused as anyone. I want it to stay together, because it's been so good. But I don't want it if it's no longer good. [Former Journey vocalist] Steve Perry said to me, 'You're right where I was when I walked away from it, and now I miss Journey'. You go like, 'Wow, I don't know if I should walk away from it'.

"I know that I'll still make records and I'll still be able to tour, but who cares about the money? That's not why I'm doing it. It's only if it's going to be fun that I'll continue with those four guys. Time will tell..."In the event, 'Blaze Of Glory' was voted 'Best Original Song' at the 1990 Golden Globe film awards, before scooping up the award for 'Best Pop/Rock Single' at the American Music Awards in January 1991. It was also nominated for the 'Best Original Song In A film' category at the 1991 Academy Awards, but was pipped at the post by film score veteran Stephen Sondheim and a song he composed for that year's much-hyped Madonna and Warren Beatty vehicle, *Dick Tracy*. It was during the Academy Awards ceremony that Jon performed 'Blaze Of Glory' in the company of Richie Sambora, in a vain bid to end growing speculation that the pair had fallen out very badly [which they had].

With no band to take out on the road, Jon threw himself into the idea of starting his own label. He already had his own production company, New Jersey Inc. "What I want to do," Jon did his best to explain at the time, "is to set up something that could be perceived as being independent in spirit. It will be distributed by PolyGram, but won't have the corporate mentality. It gives me an advantage that few other record company executives would have." He was obviously getting desperate.

Originally going to be named Underground Records, a logo for the label was even mocked up based on the London Underground logo. But eventually it was changed to Jambco (standing for Jon, Anthony, Matt Bongiovi Company. Jon's two younger brothers would be his partners in the project). The first signings were the folksy Billy Falcon and, ironically, Aldo Nova (his 'Blood On The Bricks' album would be released in 1991 to deafening silence from both critics and public alike). Old debts were being paid off, but not always for the right reasons.

Falcon's ill-fated release was lucky to see the light of day, such was the apathy that greeted its release.

But that wasn't the point with Jambco; it was there primarily to give Jon something to do while he waited to see if things could be patched up with the rest of the band. In recent times, with the band working full-time again, Jambco has predictably been put on the back burner. Aldo Nova has moved on, and at the time of writing only Billy Falcon remains signed to the label – apart, that is, from Bon Jovi themselves.

Back in 1990, the success of 'Blaze Of Glory' had clearly strengthened Jon's hand, but in a strange way it also made him realise how important Bon Jovi the band was to him. He had proved he could exist without the others, and they had proved that without him they were left floundering in the commercial wasteland. If there was a point to be made, it had been and now it was time to get over it.

Jon didn't want Bon Jovi consigned to the history books. He wanted to prove they would be around as long as they wanted to be; that there was still something to say; that there always would be.

Richie jamming at New York's China Club – without Jon.

10

" As for Richie, well there
has been a problem between us.
Look, I love Richie, but
I don't like him this week. "

ALWAYS

" It was pretty obvious
that nobody was very
happy, particularly
Jon and Richie.
The only reason they were
there was because they
were being offered a huge
amount of money. "

" We straightened
all the shit out
once and for all!
In the end, Jon and
I even went on
holiday together... "

Relationships between singers and guitarists seem eternally fraught with problems. Mick Jagger and Keith Richards of the Stones are perpetually at odds, as were The Who's Roger Daltrey and Pete Townshend. Robert Plant and Jimmy Page distanced themselves from each other for long periods in the aftermath of Led Zeppelin's crash, and it was a rift between Steven Tyler and Joe Perry that sank Aerosmith first time around. And as for Axl Rose and Slash, the future of Guns N' Roses hangs in an eternally precarious balance because of their increasingly embittered relationship. All were responsible for penning some of the most fascinating chapters in the story of rock, yet all of them have been at each other's throats, sometimes literally, during significant moments in their respective careers. The relationship between Jon Bon Jovi and Richie Sambora is no different.

They get on because they are so different. Like Jon, Richie is extremely serious about his music. Unlike Jon, he dislikes sitting in a recording studio for hours on end listening to playbacks of tracks he recorded days ago. He would rather be jamming with blues musicians in a local bar, sinking a few bevies and doing his best to forget about work for five minutes. Or maybe a bit longer.

For the most part, Jon has always accepted this, but when your energies are drained and you still have reels of tapes to listen to or plans to approve for the next day's interview schedule, or photos to look at, or whatever the hell it is everybody else wants all the time, and your partner (albeit junior partner) is off enjoying himself, sooner or later resentment starts to creep in.

That happened towards the end of the 'New Jersey' tour for sure. By the end of that trek, relations were strained to breaking point between Jon and Richie. It reached a head when Jon himself reacted to press speculation in the UK that Bon Jovi had, in fact, split up and that the general atmosphere between Jon and Richie was permanently soured.

At the time Jon told *RAW*: "As for Richie, well there has been a problem between us. Look, I love Richie, but I don't like him this week. It's not his problem, it's mine. I can't cite any reason for a rift between us because there isn't one. But don't tell me to sit at home and watch TV or take a long vacation, please! I just can't do it."

While Jon has consistently failed to set the gossip columns on fire, Richie has gained much attention, thanks to his associations with film stars Ally Sheedy and, most notably, Cher. For the most part, these have been harmless affairs that have damaged neither him nor the band. And Richie has also done much that is not publicly known. On more than one occasion, he would visit a sick fan ill in hospital without any media attention. He's a nice guy. Happy-go-lucky, perhaps a little star-struck, certainly he delights in his celebrity – but he's still the same, nice fella he was before Bon Jovi became mega-stars.

Richie's relationship with Cher (which began in 1987) added fuel to the problems between Jon and himself. Jon was happy to work with Richie on songs for Cher to record, but he never hid his personal disdain for her. These days, of course, Richie is a happily married man (see final chapter), but it didn't stop the pair spending time together as recently as May 1993, when Bon Jovi were on the road and Cher turned up at their shows in Madrid. Jon did little to disguise his intense irritation at the presence of the ageing movie queen. Just weeks before, she had interrupted the band's appearance on the much-celebrated late-night talk show, *The David Letterman Show*. Bon Jovi were playing live and just as they were about to be introduced by Letterman, Cher walked on stage unannounced and gave him a bottle of a new perfume she was promoting. It's a well-worn joke in US media circles that the host of the show has a huge crush on the surgically-enhanced songstress and her unexpected appearance on the set completely threw him. "It took the spotlight right away from us," Jon complained to one writer. "She owes me an apology for that performance." He also claimed that he would do anything to break up Richie and Cher.

The strain was increased by the fact that Richie didn't just want to play guitar, he wanted to sing and write songs, too. Until he met Jon, he'd planned on fronting his own band, and he certainly didn't lack the image or talent. "I don't have Jon's charisma, though," he once admitted to the author. "Jon's got something you can't buy; something you can't even copy, not believably. And it only comes along rarely in any walk of life, that you meet someone like that. Thankfully, whatever my own creative ambitions, I know when I'm beat, you know what I mean?"

Richie with Cher.

In 1990, though, Richie complained to friends privately that he felt increasingly stifled within the rigid Bon Jovi structure. Richie was unquestionably the No. 2 attraction in the show, contributing a substantial share of backing vocals on the big numbers like 'Wanted: Dead Or Alive', 'Livin' On A Prayer' and other hits. But it was still Jon's show and Richie was never allowed to forget that. So when Bon Jovi was unceremoniously put on ice, Richie took the chance to sign his own solo deal, determined to make an album that more accurately reflected his own musical tastes. It came out in 1991 under the title, 'Stranger In This Town'.

"Man, I can't wait for people to hear what I've done," Richie said just after finishing the record. "This isn't a Bon Jovi record at all, but rather one that allows me to take different turns and go all over the place. There's blues in here, R&B. Rock 'n' roll. Some shit that Bon Jovi could never do..."

Richie even used David Bryan and Tico Torres on his album, as if to point up his connection to Bon Jovi, while at the same time proving just how far he thought his music was from the stock-in-trade Jovi-sound. He also managed to fulfil a long-held boyhood dream by persuading Eric Clapton to trade a few guitar licks with him on the record. The pair were introduced when Richie was invited to present an award to the well-preserved bluesman in New York earlier that year, at the International Rock Awards.

Richie wrote 'Mr. Bluesman' on which Clapton plays – it's about a young kid who wants to be a guitarist and is inspired by his hero – as a special vehicle for the besuited Englishman. Richie even flew to London in March 1991 to book time at Air Studios for Clapton to lay down his solo on the song. "It's the quintessential Clapton solo – he burns," Richie still purrs at the memory. "And he's such a nice guy. He just said that when we were on stage in New York, he felt that I belonged up there with him, Buddy Guy and the others. What a compliment!"

The album was eventually released on the Mercury label, not Jambco as originally intended, a switch that came about when Richie withdrew his active support for Jon's own label. "It's true that the label was formed in the first place by Jon and myself, but having thought about it, I just decided that I didn't want to be a record company executive. I just want to concentrate on being an artist. I really just haven't got the mentality for it, I'm afraid."

All-in-all, 'Stranger...' had taken Richie nine months to complete. Neal Dorfsman, who'd worked with Dire Straits and Sting, produced, but his commitments to Dire Straits meant that the album could proceed only in fits and starts. Then Richie took three weeks out to play with Bon Jovi in Japan at the end of 1990, climaxing in a special New Year's Eve date that also featured Skid Row. "You could cut the air with a knife," remembers photographer Ross Halfin, who travelled with the band in Japan. "It was pretty obvious that nobody was very happy, particularly Jon and Richie. The only reason they were all there was because they were being offered a huge amount of money by the Japanese promoter."

When 'Stranger...' finally came out in the latter part of 1991, Richie, unlike Jon, took the chance to tour his solo album, playing clubs and small theatre dates across America. However, plans to take the show to Europe never materialised as sales of the album failed to reach expected levels, and without a hit single to give it lift, 'Stranger In This Town' was something of a flop for Richie. "I thought the title track, 'Stranger In This Town', was great," Jon once told me. "I would have liked to have done it on a Bon Jovi album, actually," he added ruefully.

As for the others... David Bryan was invited to compose the instrumental soundtrack for the low-budget horror film, *Netherworld*, released through the Full Moon label in 1991, while bassist Alec John Such much of spent his time recovering from a bad motorcycle accident.

At the end of a very long day, Jon now had enough money in the bank never to have to work again. He had a solo career just waiting to happen – if that was what he wanted – and he had his own label to develop. He also had a growing portfolio of work with other artists, including Cher, Stevie Nicks and Hall & Oates, not to mention a number of offers on the table from all quarters to get involved in outside projects. The bottom line was that he could wave Bon Jovi goodbye and be none the worse off for it, but what Jon really wanted was to put the band back together.

In early October 1991 the five members reassembled for the first time in several months. Before this there had been a series of formally arranged meetings between Jon and Richie and a qualified counsellor to help them air their grievances and repair the damage that five years of non-stop merry-go-rounding had done to their personal relationship. "It was great, we sorted all our differences out," Richie says now. "Straightened all the shit out once and for all! In the end, Jon and I went on holiday together and just started writing..."

11

" After the second album we'd pretty much had enough of chasing the latest trend. "

" We all walk in someone else's shadow at the end of the day... but that's not such a bad thing "

Could Bon Jovi work together again? That's what Jon had to find out. "We had a meeting," recalls Jon. "I said, 'We are going away for a week to talk over plans for the future'. I told my family that if I was home before Saturday then it wasn't good." The entire band retreated to the Caribbean island of St. Thomas, where they all stayed together in one house. "Just the five of us. There was only one road leading to the airport, so if anyone left they could be seen!"

Jon did his utmost to accommodate the others, but he also needed to know that they wanted to carry on as much as he did. In the end he returned home satisfied, and at the time the only five people who knew how close Bon Jovi came to splitting up were the band themselves. There was a renewed sense of purpose between the quintet. Richie's solo excursions had made him more sympathetic (despite the guitarist's protestations to the contrary) towards Jon's load.

"The guys in the band don't get their just rewards," Jon told *Metal CD* magazine in 1993. "I'll bet my nuts Tico could take any one of the guys in any of these popular bands and kick their dicks in the dirt. He's so diverse. But he doesn't get his reward, because the style of music that he's asked to play behind the songs I write, has to be a certain way. Richie's never going to be Eddie Van Halen. But he never wanted to be Eddie Van Halen. His heart was in being like Johnny Winter and Eric Clapton. He wanted to develop his style as a blues-based player – and I admire him for that.

"David, with his toes, can play better than those who beat him in the polls for 'Best Keyboard Player'. He's been playing classical music for more than 20 years. But you can't demand respect, you can't beg for respect, all you can do is survive. And that's probably the greatest testament to our work – to be around ten years, be around 15 years, come back in 20 and take a bow."

But much preparation needed to be done in order to get the 'comeback' album right on the money. And Jon wasted no time. For a start, he chose to part company with Doc McGhee. The reasons stated were, Jon announced, purely business related, but there were the usual knowing glances cast in Doc's direction.

Doc had diversified his interests, not only managing an increasing roster of bands, but becoming involved in non-music related businesses, including movies and a chain of supermarkets.

"Doc was there from the beginning and he was also a friend," says Jon. "But eventually, the fact that he has got into other businesses, while my seven days a week, 24 hours a day attitude hasn't changed, finally caught up with him." Replacing the once irreplaceable Doc proved a very difficult task for Jon. "In the end, though, I spoke to 26 managers. In fact, I got to the stage when I would talk to anyone who had something to offer. But I couldn't find the right person to suit us."

It required somebody of stature who was prepared to spend their time working solely on Bon Jovi, but it also required someone well connected who could take the band to the next level. In the end, he decided to take on the management of the band himself, forming Bon Jovi Management (BJM) with familiar faces like Paul Korzilius and Margaret Sterlacci, with whom he had worked for some years. At least he was guaranteed a managerial set-up to suit his own highly personalised aspirations; hopefully it would also have the clout to make things happen.

The long road back began in earnest in January 1992, as soon as Richie completed his US touring commitments in support of 'Stranger In This Town'. In the event, Bon Jovi ended up spending the next six months at Little Mountain Studios with famed producer, Bob Rock (The Cult, Metallica, Coverdale/Page) at the helm. "We had never spent six months before doing an album," Jon recalled. But then they had never spent a year apart before. This was to be a watershed album in the band's career, make or break time in a way it had not been since 'Slippery...' was still in conception. The result, 'Keep The Faith', justified all the added time lavished on it.

Seemingly with one confident leap, the five-piece had left behind them the pop-rock tag of the Eighties, acquiring a new respect as a truly great rock band who could transcend genres and categorisation in the burgeoning Nineties. The title track, and first single, 'Keep The Faith', was a rousing recall to arms; pop-eloquent in its touching evocation of the band's renewed commitment to each other and to their fans. The sleeve photo of five hands clutching each other conveyed a simple, familiar message from Jon, but no less potent: never give up hope, never give in.

"I wrote most of the material on the album myself," said Jon. "A lot of what's going on lyrically this time is in the first person narrative. It's not me hiding behind fictional characters, as has been the case in the past. I'm disclosing more about me than ever before."

Nothing sums this up better than 'Bed Of Roses', written by Jon when he was alone in a hotel room wondering about whether Bon Jovi had any sort of future. Jon was in an uneasy frame of mind and this is reflected beautifully in the song. The outstanding 'Dry County' is similarly evocative. Of course, there were the more uptempo and glorious vanities, such as 'In These Arms', with its instant Bon Jovi insignia, and 'Blame It On The Love Of Rock & Roll' which sounds – as its title implies – l-o-u-d. So does 'I'll Sleep When I'm Dead', in which he only half-jokingly explains why he'd rather not sit this next one out, thanks.

The world was a different place in 1992 from the one Bon Jovi had kissed farewell to, though. The optimism that the recession was about to end had given way to a certain resignation that it was here to stay – at least for the foreseeable future. And grunge, a word with no musical meaning in 1989, was now the buzz word of the music biz. Bands with a ragged attitude, musical approach and personal presentation now dominated. Nirvana and Pearl Jam were the hip bands of the moment. Glamour had been displaced by dirt, hope by fatigue, smooth production by jagged cynicism.

Bon Jovi didn't exactly bow to this trend, although Jon had his hair cut in a concerted effort to leave behind the puppy-dog pin-up paraphernalia of the past. But he wasn't about to throw everything out, just to fit in with a passing fad:

"After the second album, we'd pretty much had enough of chasing the latest trend. We calmed down and decided we were confident enough now to strip away all the bullshit and just be ourselves. And then we started to take it back and back and back, to now where it's really gotten back to a pair of jeans and a T-shirt again.

"After everything that's happened to us over the last couple of years, there isn't anything left to hide any more. It's just us being us from this point on..."

Are there any Bon Jovi influenced bands yet?

"It's already happening, man! I've already read reviews where the reviewer says some new band sounds just like Bon Jovi! Can you imagine? These kids must be puking... I remember when we got signed everybody was comparing us to Van Halen and Journey and I was puking.

"We all walk in someone else's shadow at the end of the day. But that's not such a bad thing. I see it more 'in the tradition of'..."

But the critics were hard on 'Keep The Faith'. Many openly wondered why the band were still going, seeing them as irrelevant to the Nineties. It was time, the media claimed, for them to retire. But if the press had patently failed to see Bon Jovi for what they had become, the fans were not about to make the same mistake. They bought the album in the usual vast quantities, taking worldwide sales beyond seven million, which in times of recession was quite remarkable.

And Bon Jovi quickly hit the road for an extensive tour which showed that their strength as a live band had diminished not a jot. Astutely adjusting the ticket prices in America to reflect prevailing economic conditions, the band proved a huge live draw. Moreover, they were as sharp and tight as ever.

In Europe, Bon Jovi-mania was, if anything, crazier than it had ever been. In Madrid, they needed a police motorcycle escort to and from the gig... or at least four members of the band did, Jon having gone down early to oversee operations and ensure everything was running smoothly.

Jon even took out a voice teacher on the road, determined to ensure that his vocal chords were kept in the finest trim. He has also learnt a lot about pacing. "Bruce Springsteen told me that when he was my age he never did as many shows in a row as we've been doing."

But there was little doubt that the situation in terms of workload within the band hadn't really changed much since they regrouped. However, the back-up from Richie, David, Tico and Alec was now more positive. The difficulties they encountered on a personal level seemed to have had a cleansing effect, at least in the short term.

In typical fashion, Bon Jovi found time on a pre-release promotional trip to play a Nordoff-Robbins Foundation charity show at London's Astoria Theatre, again taking the opportunity to perform their own favourite cover versions. The sight of Jon stage-diving into the audience that night was remarkable! The band had been honoured in November 1990 for their work on behalf of the Charity by being presented with the Silver Clef Award at a special lunch in New York. "We only agreed to undertake the promotional trip in the first place if we could do a gig like this at The Astoria. And we enjoyed the experience so much, just getting up there on stage and having fun. We carried on that idea when we started out on the road, just doing the occasional club show. Getting out there is what matters. "

One of the great triumphs of the entire tour came on September 18/19, when the Jovis returned to the Milton Keynes Bowl to play two sold-out dates, on a bill that also included Billy Idol, The Manic Street Preachers and Little Angels. After the first show on September 18 was announced, Jon considered the possibility of doing a free show in Hyde Park, but settled for a second date at Milton Keynes, now going under the name of the National Bowl. And 'Keep The Faith' was re-issued in the UK with a free eight-track live CD to coincide with the Milton Keynes dates.

The only fly in the ointment was some sinister rumblings from Tony Bongiovi, who tried to cash in on the success his initial investment had brought.

In late 1993, a company based in the Cayman Islands with which Tony Bongiovi was connected, started to offer around an album made up of very early John Bongiovi demos. According to his representatives, Tony Bongiovi owned the rights to these songs, and was now prepared to release them.

Altogether the tape allegedly contained some 20 songs, only two were early versions of songs that ended up on the first official Bon Jovi album – 'Runaway' and 'She Don't Know Me'. The rest were entirely unknown songs.

To date, however, no label has picked up this album for release. Why? Was Bongiovi asking too much money? Is there a doubt over the authenticity of the tape? Or had Jon got wind of this tape and somehow blocked its release?

12

ALL NIGHT LONG

66 We don't know who will be playing bass with us when we next tour... 99

66 The greatest hits thing gave us a kick up the arse... 99

Jon with Dinah Carroll at the Brits, 1994.

By the beginning of 1994, Bon Jovi were seen to be a major band in decline. Although sales of the 'Keep The Faith' album had exceeded seven million copies world-wide (not exactly insignificant), none the less in the one country that mattered most, the United States, sales had reached only two million, and it was being perceived as something of a commercial flop. The cognoscenti had spoken: Bon Jovi were yesterday's men, soon to be swept away by a tidal wave of grunge and whatever else the Nineties might throw up.

In March 1994, a new mix of 'Dry County' by Bob Clearmountain was released as a single in the UK. Just before this was put out, Jon, Richie and Tico all flew into Britain. There were two purposes to this visit. firstly, they performed the song 'I'll Sleep When I'm Dead' at the BRIT Awards, being joined on stage by Soul diva, Dinah Carroll. Secondly, Jon and Richie were to collaborate with George Martin on the George Gershwin song 'How Long Has This Been Going On', which was to appear later that year on a tribute album to harmonica-wielding legend, Larry Adler. "It was a big challenge for a rock 'n' roll player," Richie said of playing the Gershwin number. "Chord-wise Gershwin's such a different kinda thing – I had to look back at my music theory courses from college."

But of far greater interest was the absence of both David Bryan and Alec John Such. Where on earth could they be? Was there another rift in the camp? Dave's absence was easily explained. His wife was expecting twins at any moment. But what about Alec? "He got himself involved with some shit that he couldn't get out of," was Richie's deliberately enigmatic and not especially convincing explanation for the bass player's absence. Dave and Alec had been replaced, for this occasion anyway, by Aldo Nova and Meat Loaf's Kasim Sultan, respectively.

"We met Kasim on the flight over here and said, 'D'ya wanna play bass?'" was Richie's unusual explanation as to why the former Utopia man was stepping in. All of which suggested that Alec's absence was a last–minute decision. In retrospect, his absence can be seen as significant. He was never again to appear in public with Bon Jovi. The band, though, already had material ready for the next album, and were insisting that this would find them exploring new territory – both musically and geographically since Little Mountain (where they had recorded all their albums since 'Slippery...') had now closed.

"We thought we'd be like the Stones and try a place somewhere in the Caribbean," was Richie's hope. "Why beat yourself up, you know? It might make us lazy, in which case we'll split, but I don't think we're that kind of band. We realise the task ahead of us – we've gotta kick ass!"

Troubles were beginning to mount for the band, though, with reports that Bob Rock was unavailable to work on the album. Although he claimed publicly that he needed a long break from studio work, nonetheless for him to elect not to work with one of the biggest bands in the world, indicated that even he was having doubts about the band's chances of survival. And there were the rumours about Alec to deal with. His absence from the BRITs had been explained. But at one point on the 'New Jersey' tour at the end of 1993, Jon had openly admitted that the bassist had a serious alcohol problem. He had even suggested that Alec had been close to being fired. "We wanna keep the same members... Al's eccentric, but not enough to get his ass kicked out of the band!" was Richie's jovial response to probing on the vexed subject of his mysteriously missing colleague.

Alec claimed in one interview that Jon had forbidden him from doing interviews. "I was told that nobody wanted to talk to me, and that came right from Jon's mouth," he told *RAW*. "Anything they said I did I probably did, but I would lie for Jon – and I have done," he added darkly.

In the same extraordinary interview, he claimed that though he would not be involved in the next Bon Jovi album, he would be touring with them. When asked why he wasn't doing the album, he snapped: "Jon tells me I suck all the time, and I have no desire to get involved in all that tension again. They still send me tapes. I'm just very honest with them now, whereas before I guess I wouldn't have been quite so truthful."

It was totally his decision, Alec insisted. But wasn't he worried that Jon might not accept it so easily, that he might decide he didn't need him on the road with him any more, either? "I didn't think everyone would just go, 'OK'. first off, I called the guys who handle my money and asked them if I'd lose my house if that happened. They said so long as I didn't buy a yacht every week, I'd still be able to have a good life."

Tico on Alec 'leaving' the band: "Ah... you know, sometimes I think, 'It's like the old Bill Wyman syndrome'," he sighed wearily. (Wyman, bassist with The Rolling Stones for nearly 30 years, spent the last 10 of those years threatening to quit before he finally announced his retirement for good in 1992.)

"I've known Alec for 27 years, and we've been playing in bands together since we were kids. And sometimes... sometimes you get tired of doing that stuff. At the end of the day, you know, it's his decision," he said, leaving the distinct impression from the sour note in his gravel-deep voice that Tico was choosing his words carefully.

So Alec was out of the band for good then?

An even larger sigh. "Ah... I guess. We talked on the phone a little while ago and... you never can tell." Was Tico suggesting that Alec might be invited back into Bon Jovi in time for the band's live commitments this year? "You never know. I don't know. Personally, I think if your heart's not in it, you should be allowed to retire if you want. I guess that's the case with Alec.

"I mean, I hope he changes his mind. He's my friend, and if he doesn't do it I'll be pissed off," he growled. "But at the same time, you have to respect a person's feelings. Maybe Alec's just had enough."

He won't play again?

"There's a good possibility. He's into a lot of other stuff these days, production and stuff. He's even talking about starting a motorcycle shop for Harley Davidsons..."

Richie was in the limelight again in May 1994

when it came to light he was dating TV soap star Heather Locklear, until recently the wife of Mötley Crüe drummer, Tommy Lee. Tommy didn't take too kindly to this, creating a fracas outside a club in LA when he was taunted about his ex–wife's new beau. Word of Richie's latest romantic liaison 'leaked out' after Heather phoned into Howard Stern's New York radio show from her bed to tell the world – with Richie apparently snoozing beside her at the time!

But there was to be a significant upward twist in the band's fortunes during September. Bon Jovi had put together a compilation album titled 'Cross Road', to be issued during mid-October. In advance of this, a new single was issued in early September. This was the song 'Always', a new song, one of two to be featured on 'Cross Road'. The other was 'Someday I'll Be Saturday Night'. The latter was featured when Jon and Richie busked (yes, busked!) at The Piazza in Covent Garden, London, while on a visit to the city to promote the single and forthcoming album.

Before an audience of around 3,000 fans who mingled with local office workers on their lunch breaks, the pair performed 'I'll Sleep When I'm Dead', 'Prayer '94' (a new, all-acoustic version of 'Living On A Prayer'), 'Someday...', 'Wanted: Dead Or Alive' and a version of the Simon & Garfunkel classic 'Bridge Over Troubled Water'.

While Jon was in town he took time out also to announce that he was to star in a new movie *Moonlight & Valentino*, alongside Whoopi Goldberg and Elizabeth Perkins. The film was to be directed by David Anspaugh. He was to play the part of a house painter, who has a romantic interlude with Ms. Perkins' character. What had made him change his mind about finally taking a fully-fledged acting role?

"Great script, cool part... and great scheduling! I spend a month in Canada on *Moonlight...* and then go straight into the studio to begin work on the next Bon Jovi album. The timing couldn't be more perfect. Actually, I've been secretly taking acting lessons for years. I've just never chosen to speak about it before!"

It was also confirmed that the man who would produce the next Bon Jovi album would be Englishman, Peter Collins, who had already worked with the five-piece on the two new tracks. Collins has worked with some of the biggest names in hard rock, including Rush, Queensrÿche, Gary Moore, Suicidal Tendencies and Alice Cooper. "We worked with Peter on the two new tracks," Jon explained. "And when Bob Rock decided he wanted to take a year's break from producing, Peter seemed like the obvious choice." By late September, the Jovis were already far advanced in writing and pre-production for the new album, when it was revealed that Alec would not be going into the studio with them to record. He had apparently decided that he did not want to be involved in the recording process, but would still tour with them. Hardly a surprising decision given the recent publicity, but what lay behind it?

"I don't know how to answer that!" admitted Jon when confronted. "He would like to tour, but he's not doing the record. That's fine. In the studio we'll use a guy called Hugh McDonald, a session player. Alec's

focus is different. He has needs, wants and desires that are different from the other four. And we wish him well with those." Jon suggested that he wasn't totally convinced that Alec would tour with the band, but the decision rested with the bassist. Hmmm?

In early November, whilst ensconced in Bearsville Studio in upstate New York working on the new album, the Jovis announced a Summer '95 tour of European stadiums, including two dates at Wembley Stadium in London, long an ambition for Jon in particular.

Even at this point, nobody in the band would admit that Alec was out. David Bryan, who had just issued his own solo album, 'On A Full Moon', in Japan, admitted: "We actually don't know who will be playing bass with us when we tour. Hugh McDonald is playing on our next album – and he's fantastic – but whether he will come on the road with us, or Alec returns, or some third party comes in none of us are sure about.

"To be honest I'm not sure why Alec chose not to play on the new record. It was his decision totally and it mystifies me. And, no, he's not hanging out with us in the studio. Maybe it is the end of the band as we know it. We'll just have to wait and see." But the promotional posters for the tour boasted a photo of the band showing just four members – Alec had been cut out. That suggested the decision had already been taken and that Mr. Such had already gone.

Within a month, it was official. Alec John Such had 'left the band'.

"We're not hiring a replacement," explained Jon. "Because it would be too difficult a procedure. We've still no idea who will be playing bass with us when we tour next year."

So that was it. The first change to the Bon Jovi bloodline. And though for some album-buyers Bon Jovi had ceased to be a proper band some while back, nonetheless Alec's departure made it seem official. For most of their fans, though, the ones that nailed 'Always' to the world's charts for months at a time, Alec's departure meant little. In common with Guns N' Roses, who had so far lost two important guitarists and their original drummer, as long as the singer and the main guitarist were still in tow, the band were still a viable on-going good time for all.

The chances are that the bass change had even been made long before it was finally and publicly declared, and that there was a deliberate attempt to minimise the impact of the change by gradual fading Alec out of the picture. Jon was clearly hoping nobody would notice Alec had gone – and for the most part they didn't!

'Always' had reached No. 2 in Britain, and was swiftly followed-up there (where singles-buyers are known for their deep attachment to kitsch) by 'Please Come Home For Christmas'. Released as a Bon Jovi single in December '94, it had initially been recorded and released two years earlier as a Jon Bon Jovi solo performance, for inclusion on the compilation album, 'A Very Special Christmas II', all proceeds from which went to the Special Olympics Charity. Its choice as a Bon Jovi release merely underlined the increasingly

Jon prepares to busk in Covent Garden.

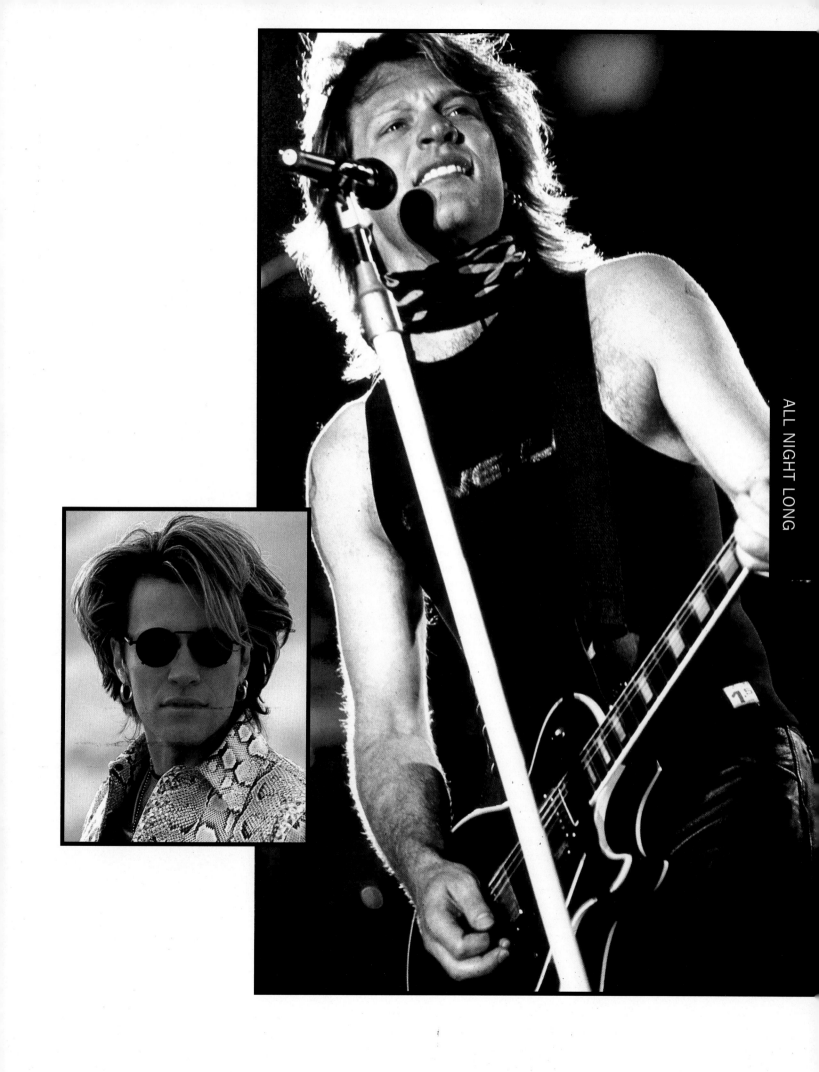

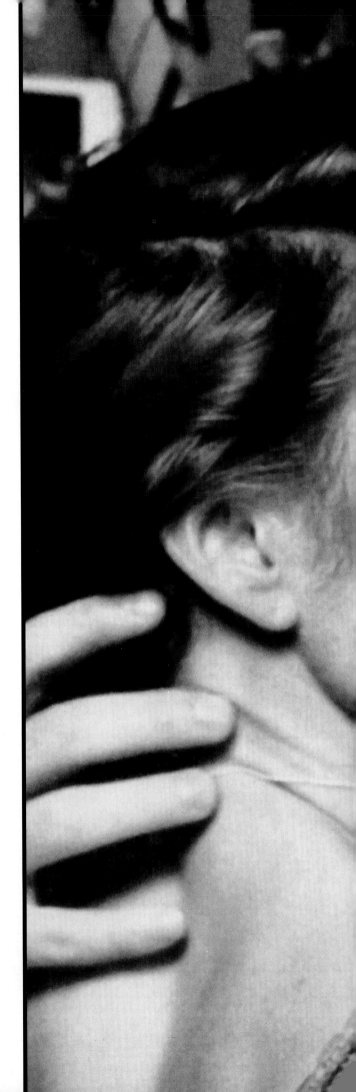

blurred lines between Jon Bon Jovi the man, and the band (whoever happens to be in it at the time) that bears his name. As if to further underline the point, Jon is the only member of the 'band' to appear in the video, smooching with supermodel Cindy Crawford.

"Basically, the story for the video is about this couple who are no longer together, and the guy is reminiscing about things. 'Course the woman he's pining over is Cindy," Jon explained, while failing to keep the grin off his face. "We were smooching for six, seven days! Forever! We had to keep doing it and doing it... It was hell! No, I'm the luckiest fucking guy in the world! Mind you, I think the video's not quite right in a few parts, so, uh, maybe we should do a reshoot?!"

Opposite: Jon with Cindy Crawford in the video for 'Please Come Home For Christmas'.

Despite Jon's protestations that Dorothea had been on the video set for the most part, some of his more impressionable female fans seemed to feel this was inconsistent with Jon's carefully manicured rock-star-next-door image. Mostly, though, no matter how old we were or what sex, we were just jealous. OK, they had put out a Christmas single to cash in on the Christmas market – but what else did we expect from Bon Jovi, at this point? A double-album?

However, none of these impressions managed to dent Bon Jovi's reinvigorated commercial appeal. 'Always' had become the band's biggest single ever in Britain. Back home in America, it reached No. 4, selling in excess of a million copies in the process. Coming off the back of their biggest hit for eight years, 'Cross Road' went straight to No. 1 in every important album chart in the world, including most of Europe, Britain, America, Japan, and Australia. By Christmas, it had already become the biggest selling album of 1994 in the UK (over a million copies sold in less than three months), and shipped more than two million copies in the US alone.

The over the top success of 'Always' and 'Cross Road' suggests that unlike many of their contemporaries from the Eighties, (Mötley Crüe, Poison, et al), Bon Jovi have escaped the grunge meltdown, and have actually gone on to become an even bigger band as a result. As Richie told the author: "The secret is the songs. A lot of bands didn't escape the Eighties because maybe they were never that great in the first place," he shrugged. "With us, it doesn't matter. You either like or hate the song first, then find out who's playing it. Not that we don't have our own sound, of course we do. But our range is broad enough now for us to write successfully in any style we want. It's what keeps us fresh."

"This greatest hits thing gave us all a kick up the ass," Torres agreed. "It gave us the confidence to keep working and experimenting. So we feel like we're ready to go now. To do things just how we want to. Even though this level of success has happened to this band before, you never expect it to keep happening every time. Never. So we're overwhelmed. It's exciting again!"

Another highlight for the band in the past couple of years was celebrating sales of 40 million

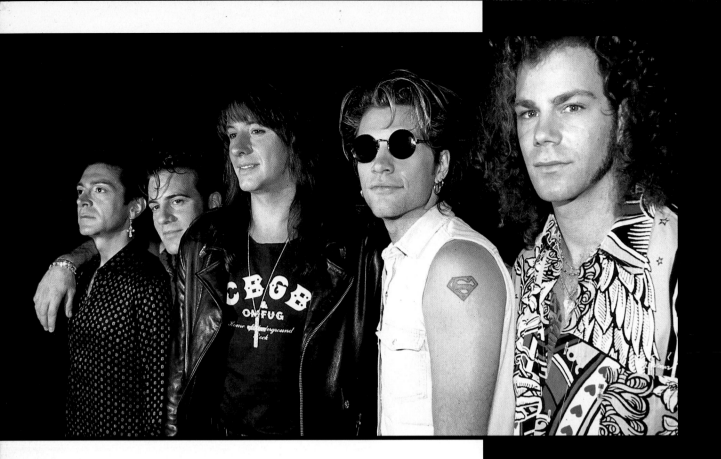

In an age of faceless stars and starless faces, Jon Bon Jovi is the exception to the rule. There is something special about him, but he doesn't flaunt it and he certainly doesn't believe it gives him the right to act in a selfish or unacceptable fashion. Most of all, though, Jon is a survivor. Bon Jovi aren't reliant on the swish of trends or the vagaries of fashion. They have carved out a niche for themselves that will not be worn away easily by the passage of time.

And 1994 ended happily enough, with Richie making at least one little girl's sweet dreams come true by marrying his girlfriend of 10 months, Heather Locklear, in Paris. Jon awaited the arrival of a second child, and Tico was stepping out with catwalk model, Eva Herzigova – better known as the Wonderbra girl!

Jon, despite his good looks and fame, was never especially promiscuous. He had dated Dorothea Hurley for several years prior to their marriage and he was keen to settle down into family life. The birth of his daughter, Stephanie Rosie, in 1993, was one of the proudest moments of his life. Talking in May of '93 whilst on tour in Europe, Jon made it plain just how much he loved Dorothea and how greatly he was looking forward to the birth of his second child, due as this book was going to press. (Jon has joked about calling it Elvis.)

"I am so proud of Dorothea. She has handled the entire pregnancy amazingly well. I just can't believe it. I want to be present at the birth. I have a private jet standing by to take me back home at a moment's notice that things are about to move. And if I can't use the jet, then I'll jump on Concorde or the first available commercial flight!"

Jon also took considerable pride in Dorothea's achievements at the US national karate championships in late 1992, when she came fourth. Domesticity seems to suit Jon to some extent – although it hasn't lowered his work rate any.

Richie has always enjoyed the company of beautiful women, in particular famous actresses. He had a brief liaison with Ally Sheedy, before beginning an affair with Cher in late 1989. Now, though, he seems to have found his soap opera princess and settled down to some extent – exactly how he'll change remains to be seen.

But what can we expect from the Jovis as the millennium winds towards its conclusion? Most would expect more changes in the line–up, and probably an increased concentration by Jon on his acting career, should *Moonlight...* – due to open in late 1995 – prove to be a success. Jon has probably bled the Jovi tanks rather dry by now, and will be sorely tempted to discard the band as a viable entity within the next couple of albums. He has his name, reputation, finances and talent intact and no longer needs to pretend to be in a gang to make an impact. Only Richie Sambora would appear to have a safe berth within the future Bon Jovi set up, and even then, who knows? Jon admitted only recently that he now feels accomplished enough to write alone, or "with anyone I like".

On the balcony of McGhee Entertainment, in the summer of 1990, with his first 'solo' record, 'Blaze Of Glory', velcroed to the No. 1 window in the US charts,

albums world-wide in their ten years plus together. This achievement was marked with a spectacular party hosted by PolyGram Records at former Beatles producer George Martin's recently opened Air Studios in north west London, actually a lavishly converted church. The place was a Gothic haven, with wine and beer on tap and giant split screens showing the classic horror movie *Lust For A Vampire*.

But even at this point in his career Jon was still a fan of great bands and great music, as he proved when talking about his abiding love for the Stones:

"When we were in Little Mountain Studios recording 'Keep The Faith', we had a giant screen erected and it was constantly playing Rolling Stones movies. That's a band who have influenced me greatly in spirit. They've written some great songs, survived anything and everything that could be thrown at them.

"I don't believe Bon Jovi can ever be what they are. Just to carry their luggage would be a privilege."

These days, Jon Bon Jovi is certainly no mere ageing heavy metal star; grunge is no longer a threat. If anything, he occupies the same position, say, Rod Stewart once occupied in the late Seventies – he's rock but he's household.

And he still loves the rock experience, especially touring:

"It's a drug, there's no doubt about it. It's the best drug I've ever done. There's just a real high about going out there and getting it together with all those people. I mean, it really works on the system. It's a really good feeling when you go out there and people smile. There's nothing like that in the whole world, man."

Jon and Dorothea.

but facing on-going problems, his ever-present credibility meter running into the red, I asked Jon Bon Jovi what he thought the next 20 years might contain for him.

He shrugged. "I don't think I can write 'Living On A Prayer' again, I know that. I just think that it is old. We did it. I think that our public is more intelligent than to expect that. I think that our organisation is more intelligent than that.

"It wouldn't be fair to us or our audience to do the same thing. I think that the songs on 'New Jersey', like 'Wild Is The Wind', which were never released as singles, are bridging the gap to where we're going."

Which is where?

"Just to do something different. I see big bands on MTV now with their new albums and it just looks and sounds like the same. That's great and all but fuck... I can't do it. It's just not right"

Would you risk your commercial impact to diversify artistically?

"Yeah, yeah... But defending Bon Jovi albums, I never in a million years thought, 'This is a commercial album, therefore it's gonna sell a lot of records'. I didn't set out to do that on 'New Jersey'. With 'Slippery...' – who knew? We had no fucking idea! And definitely not with 'New Jersey', no way.

"With this soundtrack, it's the same deal. I set out to write 10 songs. I hope you like them, end of story."

I had heard somewhere that Jon had met Prince. (This was back when he was still called 'Prince', of course.) I asked him about it.

"Prince and I met at Tramps [a London night-club] one night. We chatted over a bottle of wine – seeing Prince drunk is great."

I said I didn't know Prince drank. "He did that night!" he laughed. "He was a real sweetheart, he was great, he was funny. He was real candid. He came to see us in Minnesota."

Did he get up and jam? "Nah, he chickened out! Well, it's a whole different vibe than his kinda thing. We had rehearsed a version of 'All Along The Watchtower' at the soundcheck, but he backed out. We were ready to do it, but between the encores he said he didn't want to do it. But later that night he had an all night jam session at his studio with us and Living Colour.

"He'd invited us back to his place... we all went, it was a lotta fun. His place is ridiculous, amazing – a $10 million studio! I'd like that. I think that he is a genius lyrically and somewhat musically... I'm intrigued by guys like him. It's something different. I'd like to be responsible for going 'left'."

Would you like to work with someone like Prince?

"Yes, absolutely."

Have you discussed this with him?

"Yes."

And does he want to work with you?

"Good point. I don't know. I couldn't honestly give you an answer, so it's not fair to guess. He told us he liked our music – he came to our show, right? I mean, the idea behind working with Prince is to do something different.

"We have a couple of tracks – we never save songs usually, I throw them away – where you'd never guess it was us. One song is called 'Let's Make It Baby' and it's just about fucking. Just a nasty, Prince-style fucking song! The other one is called 'Diamond Ring', that's about what a wedding ring can do to you. It's like that song 'Fever' by Peggy Lee or something like that. It's just slinky and quiet and spooky. It doesn't have a fully fledged chorus, it's real different for us.

"With that in mind... That's where we need to go. That's where we want to go. Somewhere just a little left of where we've ever been. It might fail miserably, but at this point there's no timetable and there's no parameters which we have to keep in. So we can make an album and if it sucks then we can throw that album in the garbage and write another one.

"For the first time we have my studio which is finished now. It's a full 24-track studio. So nobody has to hear it if... it won't get stolen and sold as bootleg demos."

Richie talking to me in '94 about the songs on 'These Days': "The songs on this album pretty much all come from the time when Jon and I got back together for a while. We left all the bullshit behind and got together, just the two of us with a couple of guitars and started. And, man, it worked! Those first 40 songs came pretty quick, I can tell ya! If we hadn't stopped, we probably would have had 40 more by now... we were that tuned in to what we were doing again."

Working titles included 'Hey God' (a touch of the 'Hey Lord's perhaps?), 'Something To Believe In' (a ballad), and a rock steady memory-muncher called 'This Is A Drinking Song'.

Richie to me in '94: "I never thought we would actually break up. Never. No matter what shit we went through. I never, never thought we would ever stop. Then , when the time started slipping by and we still weren't getting it together, I always thought we would still have to get back together some day and finish this. Because it's not finished. Not yet, man. Not yet..."

Singles

She Don't Know Me/Breakout
Vertigo VER 11/*May 1984*

She Don't Know Me/Breakout
Vertigo VERX 11/*May 1984*

Runaway/Breakout (live)
Vertigo VER 14/*October 1984*

Runaway/Breakout (live)/Runaway (live)
Vertigo VERX 14/*October 1984*

In And Out Of Love/Roulette (live)
Vertigo VER 19/*May 1985*

In And Out Of Love/Roulette (live)
Vertigo VERP 19 picture disc/*May 1985*

**In And Out Of Love/Roulette (live)/
Shot Through The Heart (live)**
Vertigo VERX 19/*May 1985*

**The Hardest Part Is The Night/
Always Run To You**
Vertigo VER 22/*August 1985*

**The Hardest Part Is The Night/
Always Run To You/Tokyo Road (live)**
Vertigo VERX 22/*August 1985*

**The Hardest Part Is The Night/
Always Run To You/Tokyo Road (live)/
Shot Through The Heart (live)**
Vertigo VERDP 22/*August 1985*

**The Hardest Part Is The Night/
Tokyo Road (live)/In And Out Of Love (live)**
Vertigo VERXR 22/*August 1985*

You Give Love A Bad Name/Let It Rock
Vertigo VER26/*August 1986*

You Give Love A Bad Name/Let It Rock
Vertigo VERP 26 picture disc/*August 1986*

**You Give Love A Bad Name/
Let It Rock/Borderline**
Vertigo VERX 26/*August 1986*

**You Give Love A Bad Name/
Let It Rock/The Hardest Part Is The
Night (live)/Burning For Love (live)**
Vertigo VERXR 26 blue vinyl/*August 1986*

Living On A Prayer/Wild In The Streets
Vertigo VER 29/*October 1986*

**Living On A Prayer/Wild In The Streets/
Edge Of A Broken Heart**
Vertigo VERX 28/*October 1986*

**Living On A Prayer/Wild In The Streets/
Edge Of A Broken Heart**
Vertigo VERXP 28 green vinyl/*November 1986*

Living On A Prayer/Wild In The Streets
Vertigo VERPA 28 with free sew–on patch/
November 1986

Living On A Prayer/Wild In The Streets
Vertigo VERP 28 picture disc/*November 1986*

**Living On A Prayer/Wild In The Streets/
Only Love (live)/Runaway (live)**
Vertigo VERXG 28/*November 1986*

**Wanted: Dead Or Alive/Shot Through
The Heart**
Vertigo JOV 1/*March 1987*

**Wanted: Dead Or Alive/Shot Through
The Heart/Social Disease**
Vertigo JOV112/*March 1987*

**Wanted: Dead Or Alive/Shot Through
The Heart**
Vertigo JOVS 1 with free sticker/*March 1987*

**Wanted: Dead Or Alive/Shot Through
The Heart/Social Disease/Get Ready (live)**
Vertigo JOVR 112 silver vinyl/*April 1987*

Never Say Goodbye/Raise Your Hands
Vertigo JOV 2/*August 1987*

**Never Say Goodbye/Raise Your Hands/
Wanted: Dead Or Alive (acoustic)**
Vertigo JOV 212/*August 1987*

**Never Say Goodbye/Raise Your Hands/
Wanted: Dead Or Alive (acoustic)**
Vertigo JOVR 212 yellow vinyl/*August 1987*

Never Say Goodbye/Raise Your Hands
Vertigo JOVC 2 cassette single/*August 1987*

Bad Medicine/99 In The Shade
Vertigo JOV 3/*September 1988*

**Bad Medicine/99 In The Shade/
Lay Your Hand On Me**
Vertigo JOV 312/*September 1988*

Bad Medicine/99 In The Shade
Vertigo JOVCD 3 CD single/*September 1988*

Bad Medicine/99 In The Shade
Vertigo JOVR 3 wrap–around sleeve/
September 1988

**Bad Medicine/You Give Love A Bad Name/
Living On A Prayer (live)**
Vertigo JOVR 312/*September 1988*

Born To Be My Baby/Love For Sale
Vertigo JOV 4/*November 1988*

**Born To Be My Baby/Love For Sale/
Wanted: Dead Or Alive**
Vertigo JOV 412/*November 1988*

**Born To Be My Baby/Love For Sale/
Runaway (live)/Living On A Prayer (live)**
Vertigo JOVCD 4 CD single/*November 1988*

I'll Be There For You/Homebound Train
Vertigo JOV 5/*April 1989*

**I'll Be There For You/Homebound Train/
Wild In The Streets (live)**
Vertigo JOV 512/*April 1989*

**I'll Be There For You/Homebound Train/
Wild In The Streets**
Vertigo JOVR 512 poster sleeve/*April 1989*

**I'll Be There For You/Homebound Train/
Borderline (live)/Edge Of A Broken Heart (live)**
Vertigo JOVCD 5 CD single/*April 1989*

Lay Your Hands On Me/Bad Medicine (live)
Vertigo JOV 661 red vinyl/*August 1989*

Lay Your Hands On Me/Bad Medicine (live)
Vertigo JOV 662 white vinyl/*August 1989*

Lay Your Hands On Me/Bad Medicine (live)
Vertigo JOV 663 blue vinyl/*August 1989*

Lay Your Hands On Me/Bad Medicine
Vertigo JOV 610 shaped picture disc/
August 1989

**Lay Your Hands On Me/Bad Medicine (live)/
Blood On Blood (live)**
Vertigo JOV 612/*August 1989*

**Lay Your Hands On Me/Bad Medicine (live)/
Blood On Blood (live)**
Vertigo JOVCD 6 CD single/*August 1989*

Living In Sin/Love Is War
Vertigo JOV 7/*November 1989*

Living In Sin/Love Is War/Ride Cowboy Ride
Vertigo JOV712/*November 1989*

Blaze Of Glory/You Really Got Me Now
Jambco JBJ 1/*July 1990*

**Blaze Of Glory/You Really Got Me Now/
Blood Money**
Jambco JBJ 112/*July 1990*

Blaze Of Glory/You Really Got Me Now
Jambco JBJ MC1/*July 1990*

**Blaze Of Glory/You Really Got Me Now/
Blood Money**
Jambco JBJ CD 1/*July 1990*

Miracle/Bang A Drum
Jambco JBJ 2/*October 1990*

**Miracle/Dyin' Ain't Much Of A Livin'/
Interview**
Jambco JBJ 212/*October 1990*

Miracle/Bang A Drum
Jambco JBJ MC2/*October 1990*

**Miracle/Dyin' Ain't Much Of A Livin'/
Going Back (live)**
Jambco JBJ CD 2/*October 1990*

**Miracle/Dyin' Ain't Much Of A Livin'/
Going Back (live)**
Jambco JBJP 212/*October 1990*

**Keep The Faith/I Wish Everyday
Could Be Like Christmas**
Jambco JOV 8/*October 1992*

**Keep The Faith/I Wish Everyday
Could Be Like Christmas**
Jambco JOVMC 8/*October 1992*

**Keep The Faith/I Wish Everyday
Could Be Like Christmas/Little Bit Of Soul**
Jambco JOV CD 8/*October 1992*

**Keep The Faith/I Wish Everyday
Could Be Like Christmas/Living In Sin (live)**
Jambco JOV CB 8/*October 1992*

Bed Of Roses/Starting All Over Again
Jambco JOV 9/*January 1993*

**Bed Of Roses/Starting All Over Again/
Lay Your Hands On Me (live)**
Jambco JOV XP 9/*January 1993*

Bed Of Roses/Starting All Over Again
Jambco JOVMC 9/*January 1993*

**Bed Of Roses/Lay Your Hands On Me (live)/
Tokyo Road (live)/Ill Be There For You (live)**
Jambco JOV CD 9/*January 1993*

In These Arms/Bed Of Roses (acoustic)
Jambco JOV 10 limited edition etched
disc/*May 1993*

In These Arms/Blaze Of Glory (live)
Jambco JOV MB 10 limited edition
boxed cassette with commemorative
tour pass/*May 1993*

In These Arms/Keep The Faith (live)/
In These Arms (live)
Jambco JOV CD 10/May 1993

In These Arms/Bed Of Roses (acoustic)
Jambco JOV MC 10/May 1993

I'll Sleep When I'm Dead/
Never Say Goodbye (live acoustic)
Jambco JOV 11/July 1993

I'll Sleep When I'm Dead/
Never Say Goodbye (live acoustic)
Jambco JOV MC 11/July 1993

I'll Sleep When I'm Dead/Blaze Of Glory
(live)/Wild In The Streets (live)
Jambco JOV CD11/July 1993

I'll Sleep When I'm Dead/Blaze Of Glory
(live)/You Give Love A Bad Name (live)/
Bad Medicine (live)
Jambco JOV D11/July 1993

I Believe (Clearmountain Mix)/
I Believe (live)
Jambco JOV 12/September 1993

I Believe (Clearmountain Mix)/
I Believe (live)
Jambco JOV MC 12/September 1993

I Believe (Clearmountain Mix)/
You Give Love A Bad Name (live)/
Born To Be My Baby (live)/
Living On A Prayer (live)/
Wanted: Dead Or Alive (live)
Jambco JOV CL 12/September 1993

I Believe (Clearmountain Mix)/
Ruanway (live)/Living On A Prayer (live)/
Wanted: Dead Or Alive (live)
Jambco JOV D 12/September 1993

Dry County/Stranger In This Town (live)
Jambco JOV 13/March 1994

Dry County/Stranger In This Town (live)
Jambco JOV MC 13/March 1994

Dry County/Stranger In This Town (live)/
Blood Money (live)
Jambco JOV BX CD 13/March 1994

Dry County/It's Only Rock'N'Roll (live)/
Waltzing Matilda (live)
Jambco JOV CD 13/March 1994

Always (edit)/Always (full length)
Jambco JOV MC 14/September 1994

Always (full length)/Always (edit)/
The Boys Are Back In Town
Jambco JOV G 14/September 1994

Always (full length)/Always (edit)/
Edge Of A Broken Heart
Jambco JOV CD 14/September 1994

Always (edit)/Always (full length)/
Edge Of A Broken Heart/Prayer 94
Jambco JOV CX 14/September 1994

Please Come Home For Christmas/
I Wish Everyday Could Be Like Christmas/
Back Door Santa
Jambco JOV CD 16/December 1994

Please Come Home For Christmas/
Back Door Santa
Jambco JOV MC 16/December 1994

Please Come Home For Christmas/
Back Door Santa
Jambco JOV P 16 picture disc/
December 1994

Someday I'll Be Saturday Night/
Always (live)
Jambco JOV P 15/February 1995

Someday I'll Be Saturday Night/
Always (live)
Jambco JOV MC 15/February 1995

Someday I'll Be Saturday Night/
Good Guys Don't Always Wear White/
With A Little Help From My Friends (live)/
Always (live)
Jambco JOV CX 15/February 1995

Someday I'll Be Saturday Night/
Good Guys Don't Always Wear White/
Always (live)/Someday I'll Be Saturday
Night (live)
Jambco JOV DD 15/February 1995

Albums

BON JOVI
Runaway/She Don't Know Me /
Love Lies/Breakout/Roulette/
Shot Through The Heart/Burning For Love/
Come Back/Get Ready
Vertigo VERL 14/April 1984

7800 DEGREES FAHRENHEIT
The Price Of Love/In And Out Of Love/
Always Run To You/Only Lonely/
King Of The Mountain/The Hardest Part
Is The Night/To The fire/Silent Night/
Secret Dreams/Tokyo Road
Vertigo VERL 24/April 1985

SLIPPERY WHEN WET
Pink Flamingos/Let It Rock/
You Give Love A Bad Name /
Living On A Prayer/Wanted: Dead Or Alive/
Social Disease/Never Say Goodbye/
Wild In the Streets/I'd Die For You/
Raise Your Hands/Without Love
Vertigo VERH 38/September 1986

NEW JERSEY
Lay Your Hands On Me/
Born To Be My Baby/Bad Medicine/
Living In Sin/Wild Is The Wind/
99 In The Shade/Blood On Blood/
Homebound/Ride Cowboy Ride/
I'll Be There For You/Stick To Your Guns /
Love For Sale
Vertigo VERH 62/September 1988

KEEP THE FAITH
I Believe/Keep The Faith/
I'll Sleep When I'm Dead/In These Arms/
Bed Of Roses/If I Was Your Mother/
Dry Country/Woman In Love/Fear/
I Want You/Blame It On The Love Of
Rock & Roll/Little Bit Of Soul/
Save A Prayer
Jambco/Mercury 514 917–2/October 1992

CROSS ROAD:
THE BEST OF BON JOVI
Living On A Prayer/Keep The Faith/
Always/Wanted: Dead Or Alive/
Lay Your Hands On Me/You Give Love A
Bad Name/Bed Of Roses/Blaze Of Glory/
In These Arms/Bad Medicine/
I'll Be There For You/In And Out Of Love/
Runaway/Never Say Goodbye
Jambco/Mercury 522 936–2/October 1994

THESE DAYS